MW01054558

Midwest Living

WEEKEND GETAWAYS

UPDATED

MIDWEST LIVING Weekend Getaways
Project Editors: Barbara Humeston, Mark Ingebretsen
Graphic Designer: Mick Schnepf
Assistant Editors: Ira Lacher, Linda Ryberg
Contributor: George Hendrix
Map Illustrator: Mike Burns

MIDWEST LIVING Magazine
Editor: Dan Kaercher
Managing Editor: Barbara Humeston
Art Director: Richard Michels

Meredith Publishing Group
President: Christopher M. Little
Vice President, Consumer Marketing & Development: Hal Oringer

Meredith Corporation
Chairman and Chief Executive Officer: William T. Kerr
Chairman: E. T. Meredith III

Cover: Door County, Wisconsin *(see page 18)*
Photograph: Wm. Hopkins/Hopkins & Associates

L ooking for an easygoing weekend adventure? Twenty great possibilities are right at your fingertips in this new auto-tours guide. We've packaged terrific mini-vacations in some of our favorite areas of the Midwest, complete with trip mileage and routing instructions, restaurants and accommodations recommendations, and must-see sights and attractions along the way.

Most of the tours range from 150 to 250 miles, so you won't spend your whole weekend behind the wheel. The destinations vary from the rugged north shore of Lake Superior in Minnesota to Mark Twain's storied haunts along the Mississippi and the gentle, rolling, rural landscapes of Ohio's Amish country.

Each tour includes a basic route map, but we recommend starting out with a good road atlas or a current state road map as well. Though we've highlighted stops on each weekend route, you're certain to make your own discoveries along the way. That's part of the fun on these take-it-easy tours!

If you can't travel one of our complete weekend routes, keep our guide handy in your glove box whenever you're driving in the Midwest. There's almost certain to be a town, attraction, restaurant or lodging not far from wherever you're going.

We hope each of our weekends turns out to be just the kind of getaway you've been seeking. We'd love to hear your comments about our auto-tours guide. Write to us at: *Great Weekend Getaways, MIDWEST LIVING®, 1716 Locust St., Des Moines, IA 50309-3023.* Safe and happy traveling!

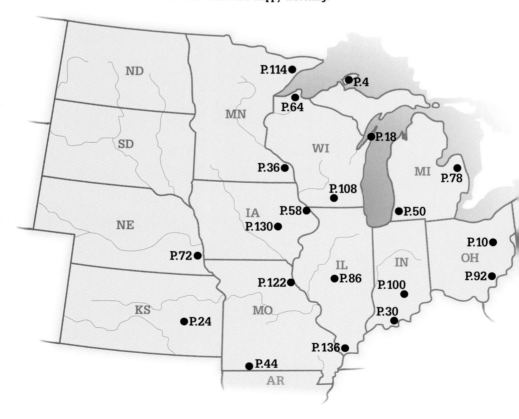

CONTENTS

SPLENDORS OF THE KEWEENAW PENINSULA

Just 100 miles long and 30 miles wide, the Keweenaw Peninsula might seem tiny compared with the rest of Michigan's vast Upper Peninsula (UP). But this finger of land jutting into Lake Superior from the north shore of the UP casts a unique spell on visitors. Winding ribbons of roads lead to agate beaches, rugged shoreline, inland lakes and streams, and vast, pristine forests that are playgrounds for wildlife.

Abandoned mining towns stand as reminders of the peninsula's past. Miners, including many Finns and other immigrants, first came to the Keweenaw in search of copper 150 years ago. They built ethnic churches and ornate mansions, leaving behind traditions that remain an important part of peninsula life.

Today, visitors explore little harbor and mining towns, and savor the scenery and mystical silence of the north woods. They climb the hills, prowl the lakeshores, bike, camp, hike the trails to waterfalls and sail away on sunset cruises.

This loop tour leads you along 165 miles of scenic roadways. Starting in the gateway town of Houghton, you'll follow Portage Lake. Dredged in the 1850s to create a watery highway for vessels hauling copper ore, the lake cuts through the peninsula's base. The route travels from Chassell, on Portage Lake's south shore, to Freda, overlooking Lake Superior. You venture to the Keweenaw's tip and explore the village of Copper Harbor, discovering still more of the Keweenaw's treasures along the way.

Eagle Harbor's lighthouse, guiding ships on Lake Superior.

-------- **1** --------
Houghton

(Population: 7,500) Houghton and its sister town, Hancock *(see No. 3)*, face each other from 500-foot rises across Portage Lake. Two- and three-story homes snuggle into hillsides among the church steeples. The Portage Lift Bridge rises like an elevator to allow boats to pass below.

The sidewalk along Portage Lake is just right for strolling. Stop at one of several mini-parks along the way and watch the boat traffic, including *Ranger III,* the ferry that carries visitors to Isle Royale National Park.

Houghton is the home of Michigan Tech University. On the campus, the Seaman Mineralogical Museum holds more than 30,000 mineral specimens that together help trace the region's geological history. You'll discover many of these stones in the wilds of this mineral-rich peninsula.

In town, pay a visit to Keweenaw Gem and Gift. The store stocks native copper creations, gems and Isle Royale greenstone. The Windigo, a gift shop along Shelden Avenue, stocks everything from lighthouse prints to art nouveau jewelry.

Drive 7 miles south on US-41.

-------- **2** --------
Chassell

(Population: 730) A scattering of storefronts, homes and a couple of gas stations signal that you've reached Chassell on Portage Lake's south shore. Residents sometimes set antiques out on their porches for passing visitors to buy. Make a stop at The Einerlei, a store that combines country gifts and dried-flower wreaths with a backyard herb garden.

Just south of downtown, lookout towers provide views of the marsh in the Sturgeon River Slough Natural Area. It's a rest stop for migrating geese and ducks.

You can pick your own strawberries at nearby farms or pull up at stands that dot the roadsides in season.

Backtrack 7 miles to Houghton on US-41. Bypass the Portage Lift Bridge,

Lake Superior laps at the peninsula's shore.

DAN URBANSKI

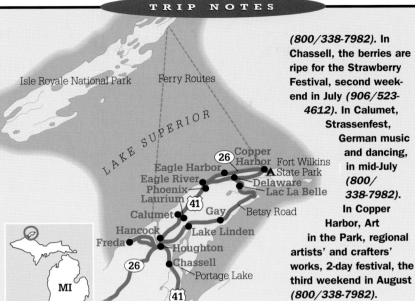

Isle Royale National Park

Ferry Routes

LAKE SUPERIOR

26 Copper Harbor
Eagle Harbor
Eagle River
Phoenix
Laurium
Calumet 41 Gay
Hancock
Freda
Lake Linden
Houghton
26 Chassell
Portage Lake
41

Fort Wilkins
State Park
Delaware
Lac La Belle
Betsy Road

MI

(800/338-7982). In Chassell, the berries are ripe for the Strawberry Festival, second weekend in July **(906/523-4612).** In Calumet, Strassenfest, German music and dancing, in mid-July **(800/338-7982).** In Copper Harbor, Art in the Park, regional artists' and crafters' works, 2-day festival, the third weekend in August **(800/338-7982).**

CHARTER FISHING—In Mohawk, Lucky Strike Charter Fishing. In Calumet, Goin' Trolling Guide Service. In Copper Harbor, Fred's Charters.

SIDE TRIP—Houghton and Copper Harbor are gateways to 45-mile-long Isle Royale, the largest of 200 islands that make up Isle Royale National Park, (165 miles of trails, scuba diving at 10 shipwreck sites, wildlife-watching, fishing and north-woods scenery). You can overnight at campsites or at Isle Royale's Rock Harbor Lodge (reservations required; doubles from $223, including meals). *Isle Royale National Park, 87 N. Ripley St., Houghton, MI 49931 (906/482-0984).*

INFORMATION—*Keweenaw Tourism Council, 1197 Calumet Ave., Calumet, MI 49913 (800/338-7982).*

TOUR ROUTE—A 165-mile tour, laced with forest and lake views, plus stops in harbor towns and mining communities.

LODGINGS—Standard motels in Houghton, Hancock and Copper Harbor. Other choices: In Houghton, Best Western King's Inn Motel, indoor pool (doubles from $53); Franklin Square Inn, overlooking Portage Lake (doubles from $72). In Laurium, the 1908 Laurium Manor Inn, an art nouveau bed and breakfast (doubles from $69). In Eagle Harbor, Eagle Harbor Inn, eight rooms, four blocks from a sandy beach (also hearty home cooking; doubles from $42). In Copper Harbor, Keweenaw Mountain Lodge, one- to three-bedroom cabins and motel units (doubles from $65); Lake Fanny Hooe Resort, motellike lodgings (doubles from $60).

CAMPING—F.J. McLain State Park, north of Hancock. Fort Wilkins State Park, east of Copper Harbor.

DINING—In Houghton, The Library Bar & Restaurant, from hearty soups to steaks; 3 miles south of town along US-41, Onigaming Supper Club, fine views of Portage Lake. In Hancock, Kaleva Cafe, a locals' spot (check out the pastry case by the door). In Laurium, Toni's Country Kitchen for pasties (sandwich-size meat-and-potato pies) and Finnish baked goods. In Eagle Harbor, Shoreline Restaurant, home-style cooking (known for delicious pies).

CELEBRATIONS—In Houghton, the Bridge Fest and Seafood Fest, party on a parking deck overlooking the Portage Lift Bridge, Father's Day weekend in June

and take Canal Road north. Then, turn west on Liminga Road, making a 39-mile loop. The ridges of Oskar Bay overlook Portage Lake and expanses of farmland. Turn west on Liminga Road to Freda, then return on Covered Road through a hardwood forest. Cross the bridge to Hancock.

Hancock

(Population: 5,120) In this 18th-century copper-mining town, many of the vintage buildings seem to be natural outgrowths of the steep hillsides. Suomi College, the only Finnish-American college in the nation, welcomes visitors. Its Finnish-American Heritage Center houses one of the best collections of Finnish-American literature and art in North America.

At the top of Quincy Hill, the Keweenaw Waterways Overlook provides a sweeping view. The structure dominating the skyline is the 150-foot-tall shaft house at the Quincy Mine Hoist. The building serves as a tribute to all the copper miners who worked (sometimes more than 1½ miles deep) in one of the world's richest copper mines. From the museum there, you can take an underground mine tour.

Both the hoist and the museum are part of Keweenaw National Historical Park. One of our newest national parks, it's dedicated to preserving the peninsula's mining heritage. The park encompasses several Keweenaw sites (get a tour map at the Keweenaw tourism office in Calumet).
Drive 11 miles north on US-41.

Calumet

(Population: 1,010) Calumet's old homes show influences of Gothic and Romanesque architecture. At the tourism office along Calumet Avenue, you can pick up a brochure that details a walking tour. Be sure to visit the Coppertown USA Mining Museum, with its simulated mine and hands-on exhibits. Browse or buy at the Copper Art Store, where artisans create ornamental art from sheet copper. Stop by the Historic Calumet Theatre. The ornate, sandstone opera house, built during the bullish mining era, now hosts major touring productions, as well as community events.
Cross US-41 to your next stop.

Laurium

(Population: 2,680) Bric-a-brac-trimmed mansions that copper mining bosses built line Laurium's quiet streets. The largest home in town, now the Laurium Manor Inn, a bed and breakfast, gives tours.

Nearby, have a look at the monument to famous Laurium native George Gipp, the real "Gipper."
Drive 14 miles north on US-41 past once-thriving mining communities, including the settlement of Phoenix. All have long since become ghost towns except for visitors who stay in several restored cabins. From Phoenix, drive about 2 miles northwest on State-26.

Eagle River

(Population: 20) For a glimpse at the harsh lives early Keweenaw settlers led, stroll through the Evergreen Cemetery and read the sad epitaphs on the tombstones. From the river bridge, you can see water cascading over a wooden dam.
Drive 8 miles northeast on State-26. On the way, watch for the Jam Pot, a store at Jacob's Creek Falls. Monks pick local berries and turn them into jams and jellies you can buy.

Eagle Harbor

(Population: 50) Beaches line sheltered waters of Eagle Harbor. The tiny town was named after Eagle Harbor Mining Company, which operated here more than a century ago. Stop by Eagle Harbor Store, an old general store. The Catholic church, built in 1852, still serves a small congregation.
Drive 12 miles northeast on State-26, passing agate-strewn beaches along the way. Turn right at the second sign for Brockway Mountain for a 4-mile scenic drive high above the lake. Return to State-26 over the same route.

Copper Harbor

(Population: 70) Almost everything is one of a kind in Copper Harbor, a town

Fort Wilkins State Park at the peninsula's tip.

DAN URBANSKI

with one general store, as well as one fudge shop, museum, ice cream shop, golf course, state park, lighthouse and school. Lodgings and restaurants are in far greater abundance.

You can browse and buy at the Laughing Loon gift shop and at Country Village Shops (ask fourth-generation owner Barbara Foley if you can sample the thimbleberry fudge). Waitresses at the Harbor Haus restaurant rush dockside to dance a can-can when the *Isle Royale Queen III* returns from daily passenger service to Isle Royale National Park, 48 miles beyond the peninsula's shore.

At Fort Wilkins State Park, visitors can tour a wooden frontier fort, the only one of its kind east of the Mississippi River. Built in 1844, the complex includes 16 restored buildings, a lighthouse and the remains of Michigan's first commercial copper mine. Costumed interpreters help you relive the fort's colorful heyday.

Drive 11 miles southwest on US-41, a designated Scenic Highway framed by white birch and hardwood trees.

Delaware

The Delaware Copper Mine conducts tours down to its first level, 110 feet below the surface. Topside, abandoned houses stand silent along the deserted dirt streets of this ghost town.

Drive 5 miles southeast from Delaware on Lac La Belle Road to Lac La Belle. Follow Betsy Road east, then south 22 miles to Gay. Drive Gay Road 12 miles west to Lake Linden. The route makes a circle to Lake Linden and back to State-26, with waterfalls, picnic areas and beaches on the way.

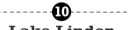
Lake Linden

(Population: 1,203) Slide into one of the wooden booths at Lindell's Chocolate Shop, an old-time confectionery. Nearby, the Houghton County Historical Museum exhibits mining artifacts and local memorabilia.

Drive 11 miles southwest on State-26 to complete your tour. ■

By Dixie Franklin.

9

EXPLORING AMISH BYWAYS

Just as the highways narrow and strike off among farm fields and pastures, distinctive road signs begin to appear. The yellow, diamond-shaped signs, emblazoned with black horse-and-buggy silhouettes, send both a warning and a promise to motorists: You're in Ohio's Amish country; take it slow.

Time travels at a clip-clop pace throughout the rolling rural landscapes of northeast Ohio. Cleveland lies just 1½ hours north and Columbus just 1½ hours southwest, but their big-city lifestyles haven't invaded Holmes County, the heart of Ohio Amish country and where this tour begins. Some 30,000 Amish live here, making up the largest of the religious group's communities in the U.S.

Towns such as Millersburg, Berlin and Walnut Creek may bustle with shops, eateries and weekend visitors. But turn off the main roads, and buggies outnumber cars. Two-lane highways meander past teams of stout Belgian draft horses working the fields. You pass tidy, white farmhouses, one-room schools, spinning windmills, and home-sewn dresses dancing on clotheslines. Hand-lettered signs in front of the homes advertise Amish-made butter, farm-fresh eggs and other goods for sale.

Amish country is rich in history, and many groups, in addition to the Amish, have taken part in its saga. The peaceful village of Zoar preserves a 19th-century religious commune. Schoenbrunn Village shows you how early pioneers made their homes in the New World. In Coshocton, a mid-1800s canal town comes to life at Roscoe Village. And always, along the twisting roads on this 165-mile tour, the ever-present Amish country signs remind you: You'll see much more when you travel at a horse-and-buggy pace.

Amish families head to worship in the farm country of northeast Ohio.

❶ Millersburg

(Population: 3,100) Forested hills frame this county-seat town in the heart of Amish country. A stroll along Jackson Street, Millersburg's main thoroughfare, reminds you of a downtown scene in some old, black-and-white movie. Businesses operating behind turn-of-the-century storefronts sell hardware and baked goods, as well as Amish crafts.

Traffic crawls behind buggies transporting Amish families to town for supplies or to do business at the courthouse towering over the square. For many Amish families, these trips to town also are opportunities to keep in touch with their neighbors.

Down the street, the restored three-story Hotel Millersburg, built in 1847, welcomes visitors again. Four blocks north along State-83, you can tour the Victorian House, a 28-room Queen Anne mansion. A Cleveland industrialist built the house for his wife and 12 children in 1900. The mansion's furnishings, wall coverings and draperies all are authentic to their era.
Drive 7 miles east on US-62.

❷ Berlin

(Population: 3,000, in the area) Shops selling Amish quilts, furniture and knick-knacks have taken over this tiny town the locals pronounce as BURR-len. The Yankee Workshop sells pottery, baskets and folk art in Berlin's oldest house. At the Helping Hands Quilt Shop down the street, hundreds of quilts stack neatly on shelves.

Money from sales goes to Amish and Mennonite charities. The two groups share common roots and maintain close ties.

Just east of town along State-39, Jo Ann Hershberger, a Mennonite whose grandfather was an Amish bishop, greets visitors at Shrock's Amish Farm. There, you can take a ride in an authentic black buggy and tour an authentic Amish home.
Drive 2 miles east on US-62 and 5 miles north on County-77.

Amish frequent small towns throughout the region.

DOYLE YODER

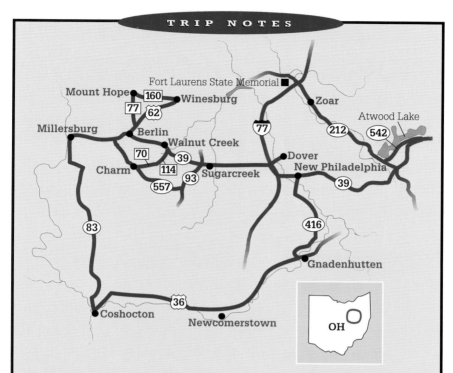

TOUR ROUTE—A 165-mile loop through northeast Ohio's Amish country, also visiting some of Ohio's historic sites.

LODGINGS—Standard motels around Berlin, New Philadelphia and Coshocton. Other choices: In Millersburg, Hotel Millersburg, rooms with handcrafted Amish quilts (doubles from $49). Near Millersburg, The Inn at Honey Run for pampering contemporary lodgings (also elegantly prepared fare; doubles from $74). In Walnut Creek, Carlisle Village Inn, Victorian-style rooms (doubles from $84). Near Charm, Charm Countryview Inn, owned by a Mennonite family, rooms decorated with Amish furnishings (doubles from $75). In Coshocton, Roscoe Village Inn, Shaker-style furnishings (also great dining; doubles from $85). Near New Philadelphia, modern, full-service Atwood Lake Resort, with golf course (doubles from $115).

DINING—In Walnut Creek, Der Dutchman, hearty Amish cooking and from-scratch pie. In Sugarcreek, The Swiss Hat for stick-to-the-ribs Amish fare. In Coshocton, Old Warehouse Restaurant, rich desserts and yesteryear atmosphere.

CAMPING—Atwood Lake Park, south of Atwood Lake along State-542. Amish Country Campsites along US-62, north of Winesburg. Whispering Hills Campgrounds, 10 miles west of Millersburg along State-515, off State-39.

CELEBRATIONS—East of Berlin, Berlin Pioneer Festival, crafters and artists sell their works (100 booths), two weekends in September (330/893-1700). In Zoar, Harvest Festival, classic-car show and crafters' booths, first weekend in August (330/874-3011).

INFORMATION—*Ohio Div. of Travel & Tourism, Box 1001, Columbus, OH 43216 (800/BUCK-EYE); Holmes County Chamber of Commerce, 5798 County-77, Millersburg, OH 44654 (330/674-3975); Amish Country Visitors Bureau, Box 177, Berlin, OH 44610 (216/893-3467); Tuscarawas County Convention & Visitors Bureau, Box 926, 101 E. High, New Philadelphia, OH 44663 (800/527-3387); Coshocton County Convention & Visitors Bureau, Box 905, Coshocton, OH 43812 (800/338-4724).*

---------**3**---------
Mount Hope

(Population: 230) Wednesdays are sale days at the cavernous auction house in Mount Hope. Brace yourself for a traffic jam. Buggies, laden with pies and breads carefully packed for sale, poke along behind wagons crowded with squealing pigs or swaying under loads of hay.

On sale day, an open-air flea market surrounds the auction house. You can buy everything here—from fresh produce to antique farm tools. Inside the auction house, Amish men, listening gravely, have no trouble following the auctioneer's breakneck spiel, raising a finger to bid on a load of eggs or a spindly-legged calf.

Nearby, the Amish tie up their horses in front of Lehman's Hardware, chief supplier of all the necessities of life in a world without electricity. This store brims with items other hardware stores stopped selling generations ago: copper washtubs, oil lamps and cedar butter churns. A blacksmith, harness-repair and buggy-making shop also serve Amish customers.

Drive 5 miles east on County-160 to Winesburg. Winesburg Collectables, a converted general store that now sells antiques and Amish crafts, makes a worthwhile stop. Then, drive 6 miles southwest on US-62 and 4 miles east on State-39.

---------**4**---------
Walnut Creek

(Population: 3,000, in the area) Visitors flock to tiny Walnut Creek for home-style cooking at Der Dutchman, the area's largest Amish restaurant. The main dining room overlooks rolling farmland. You can walk to neighboring shops, including a Victorian home that houses Coblentz Chocolates, where you can watch candy-makers hand-dip their rich confections. Buy some treats to take home.

Drive 4 miles south on County-114, then continue 2 miles west on County-70.

---------**5**---------
Charm

(Population: 2,800, in the area) Amanda Miller's quilt shop, along the main street, began attracting visitors to this Holmes County town more than 30 years ago. In those days, the soft-spoken Amish woman sold only traditional, dark-colored Amish quilts from her white-clapboard cottage. But today, bright paisley and calico quilts in almost every imaginable pattern hang from the walls and ceiling.

Drive 6 miles southeast on State-557, then drive 4 miles north on State-93 and 1 mile east on State-39.

---------**6**---------
Sugarcreek

(Population: 2,100, in the area) Alpine murals decorate the facades of businesses in this farming community. Homes built to look like Swiss chalets stand beneath giant grain-storage bins. Sugarcreek is known as the "Little Switzerland of Ohio" (13 Swiss cheese factories operate nearby). Milk for the cheese comes from local Amish farms. Downtown bakeries and craft shops also lure visitors. The Ohio Central Railroad's vintage steam train departs from Sugarcreek's historic depot along Factory Street for 1-hour trips through the countryside (May–October).

Continue 8 miles east on State-39.

---------**7**---------
Dover

(Population: 11,700) Another town with a Swiss heritage, Dover makes a good, short detour from your route. Visitors come to this farming community to tour the Warther Museum, where master carver Ernest Warther's works trace the history of steam locomotives. The museum holds 64 working model locomotives carved from ebony and ivory, including one with 10,000 parts that took the carver more than 20,000 hours to complete.

You also can tour the opulent J.E. Reeves Home & Museum, a 17-room Victorian mansion.

Backtrack 1 mile to I-77 and drive 12 miles north and northeast to exit 93.

---------**8**---------
Fort Laurens
State Memorial

Fort Laurens State Memorial marks the site of Ohio's only Revolutionary War outpost. The 82-acre grounds make a nice picnic spot. A museum features

At many Amish farms, you can buy crafts and treats to eat.

exhibits about the Revolutionary War. *Drive 3 miles southeast on State-212.*

--------- **9** ---------

Zoar

(Population: 170) In 1817, more than 200 German immigrants fleeing religious persecution founded this village on the banks of the Tuscarawas River. These separatists called the village Zoar, meaning "refuge."

The utopian community disbanded in the late 1800s, but today's residents keep the town's heritage alive. More than 40 of the settlement's original buildings still stand—many completely restored (eight are open to visitors). Start your tour at the Garden of Happiness. The floral display depicts Zoar's religious philosophy and fills the entire town square.

The Number One House, dating to 1835, displays Zoar furniture and crafts. The Zoar Store sells artful reproductions of 19th-century antiques. In the Meeting House, the 100-year-old organ still plays for worshipers who sit on the same wooden benches Zoar's founders used.

Drive about 15 miles southeast on State-212 to Atwood Lake, popular for sailing, swimming and hiking. Follow State-542 along the lake to get to Atwood Lake Park or Atwood Lake Resort, both worthwhile stops. Drive 20 miles back southwest on State 39.

--------- **10** ---------

New Philadelphia

(Population: 15,700) Moravian missionaries came to the New Philadelphia area in 1772. The village they founded, Schoenbrunn, means "beautiful spring." But these settlers' hopes for a peaceful life in their new land were dashed by the Revolutionary War and the slaughter of 96 of the missionaries' Native American followers by renegade Americans.

Schoenbrunn Village State Memorial re-creates this first settlement with 17 log buildings. Nearby, *Trumpet in the Land,* Pulitzer Prize-winning playwright Paul Green's outdoor drama, retells the story of the early Moravians (mid-June to late August). You almost forget that you're watching a play as the guns blaze and the horses gallop across the stage.

Drive 10 miles south on State-416 and less than 1 mile east on US-36.

--------- **11** ---------

Gnadenhutten

(Population: 1,320) The name of this settlement means "tents of grace"—ironic, because the tragedy that *Trumpet in the Land* depicts took place here. A historical park and museum mark the Indians' burial site.

Drive 29 miles west on US-36. Stop en route at Newcomerstown, where the Temperance Tavern Museum, once an Ohio-Erie Canal stop, tells the story of two Ohio sports immortals: baseball's Cy Young and football's Woody Hayes.

--------- **12** ---------

Coshocton

(Population: 12,200) Set at the confluence of three rivers, Coshocton boomed when the Ohio-Erie Canal opened in 1825. Trains eventually replaced the canal boats, but Roscoe Village, a living-history settlement just north of town off State-16/83, recaptures the canal era's heyday with Greek Revival storefronts, brick sidewalks and wrought-iron lampposts.

Visitors flock to museums, shops and restaurants along the village's main thoroughfare, Whitewoman Street. A blacksmith, weaver and other costumed interpreters labor in the shops and homes.

At the Roscoe General Store, there's even a real cracker barrel amid toys, kitchenware, gifts and penny candy. The nearby Canal Carver specializes in folk art: rabbits, Santas and such made from wood and clay. Be sure to drop by Captain Nye's Sweet Shop & Cafe, a cozy ice cream parlor (try the fudge).

For still more glimpses of canal-era life, stop in at the Visitors Center Exhibit Hall, filled with miniature dioramas depicting canal-building days. Then, stroll over to the old canal. From there, you can board the *Monticello III,* a canal boat that plies the waterway, once a vital transportation link. A horse pulls the boat along, just as horses pull the black buggies you see exploring Amish byways.

Drive 24 miles north on State-83, returning to Millersburg to complete your tour. ∎

By Barbara Briggs Morrow.

On backroads, traditional Amish buggies often outnumber the cars.

THE MAGIC OF DOOR COUNTY

More than 250 scenic miles of shore outline the rolling, forested sliver of land that's Wisconsin's northeast corner. Jutting northward between Green Bay and Lake Michigan, water defines the Door Peninsula, a realm of gleaming-white villages, beckoning beaches, and mirrorlike bays dotted with sailboats. In fact, you're never more than 10 minutes from a view of the lake or the bay.

Door County takes its name from Porte de Morts Passage (Death's Door), the treacherous strait at the peninsula's tip that links Green Bay's protected waters with the rough, open waters of Lake Michigan. Locals talk of "lake side" and "bay side" when they give directions and when they describe the peninsula.

On the bay side, or northwest shore, you'll discover Door County's most popular towns, bustling on summer weekends with visitors browsing through art galleries, sampling fudge, and exploring shops and restaurants. The lake side, or southeast shore, strikes visitors as far more rugged, showcasing the peninsula's natural beauty with long stretches of white-sand beach and rocky cliffs pounded by surf. Inland, you'll discover gently rolling rural countryside and the county's celebrated cherry orchards.

This 90-mile route samples the best of this compact area's many sights and attractions, including a ferry trip to Rock Island, just off the peninsula's tip. The route begins and ends in Sturgeon Bay, the unofficial gateway to the peninsula.

Ephraim, a
New Englandlike
village along
Green Bay.

----------❶---------- Sturgeon Bay

(Population: 9,180) Driving over the State-42/57 bridge, you may spot enormous freighters or tankers crossing below. Sturgeon Bay's own shipyards lie along the canal banks to the north, and the city spreads out northeast of the canal. Downtown Sturgeon Bay boasts a large historic district of stores and Victorian-era homes. You can shop at the White Birch Inn for Native American art and at the Pottery House for ceramics. Tour, taste and buy at the Cherryland Brewery in the renovated train station.

Drive 17 miles north on State-42 across the peninsula's interior, passing through Carlsville. You can stop at the Peninsula Winery there, which gives tours to visitors.

----------❷---------- Egg Harbor

(Population: 180) The deep, well-protected waters off Egg Harbor make it a favorite anchorage of summer sailors. Family resorts cluster around this vacation town, set on a bluff. Students from the nearby Birch Creek Music Center often perform free concerts in the gazebo at the historic Cupola House. Browse the Robert Leland Pence Gallery, where the artist displays his paintings of Door County landscapes. A couple of miles south along County-G, you'll discover Murphy County Park, with a great swimming beach and picnic area.

Drive 6 miles north on State-42.

----------❸---------- Fish Creek

(Population: 250) One of the peninsula's more bustling commercial areas, Fish Creek becomes Door County's social and cultural hub each summer with a crowded calendar of music and theater events. The schedule includes performances by the Peninsula Players, among America's oldest resident summer stock companies. The curtain rises on the troupe's plays every night (except Monday) in a garden theater.

You'll also discover some of the

Fish-boil time at the White Gull Inn in Fish Creek.

BUCK MILLER

TOUR ROUTE—90 miles, skirting Door County Peninsula's shore, visiting towns, beaches and preserves.

LODGINGS—Standard motels throughout the peninsula. Other choices: In or near Sturgeon Bay, Bay Shore Inn, a lodge with a massive stone fireplace, along Green Bay (suites from $165); White Lace Inn, Victorian decor (doubles from $98). In or near Egg Harbor, Egg Harbor Lodge, modern rooms with Green Bay views (doubles from $95); Alpine Inn and Cottages, a 300-acre resort (doubles from $69). In Fish Creek, White Gull Inn (doubles from $99) and neighboring Whistling Swan (doubles from $99, including breakfast), both historic lodgings. Near Cana Island, Gordon Lodge, motel units and cabins on a secluded point (doubles from $100, with breakfast). Near Sister Bay, Little Sister Resort, a cottage resort (from $340 per adult per week with two meals daily). Along Rowleys Bay, Wagon Trail Resort, lodge rooms and homes in the woods (doubles from $109).

CAMPING—In Peninsula State Park (reserve in writing after January 1). Potawatomi State Park, northwest of Sturgeon Bay. East of Ellison Bay, Newport State Park (backpackers only).

DINING—In Sturgeon Bay, the Inn at Cedar Crossing for Door County delicacies such as capered whitefish and pan-seared pork loin. In Fish Creek, the White Gull Inn, fish boils and a breakfast locals call the best in town; the Cookery, breakfast specials, baked goods and homemade soups (try the whitefish chowder). In Sister Bay, Al Johnson's Swedish Restaurant, Swedish pancakes with lingonberries and meatballs. In Baileys Harbor, Weisgerber's Cornerstone Pub, downhome tavern setting and pan-fried perch dinners on Friday nights.

CELEBRATIONS—Throughout the county, Door County month-long Festival of Blossoms, in May (920/743-4456). In Ephraim, Fyr Bal Festival, celebrating the town's Scandinavian heritage, mid-June (920/854-2515). In Fish Creek, Peninsula Music Festival attracts symphony devotees from across the Midwest, several weeks in August (920/854-4060).

SPECIAL NOTE—Summer crowds often jam Door County's roads on weekends. Plan a weekday summer visit or come in late spring or early fall.

INFORMATION—*Door County Chamber of Commerce, Box 406, Sturgeon Bay, WI 54235 (920/743-4456); Wisconsin Dept. of Tourism, Box 7976, Madison, WI 53707 (800/432-8747).*

area's best shopping here, including the chic shops at Founder's Square.

At the White Gull Inn, another nightly summer spectacle takes place: an authentic Wisconsin fish boil (reservations recommended). Like the many other Door County restaurants that host fish boils, the inn begins with a large, open-air fire. Cooks toss potatoes, onions and whitefish steaks into a huge kettle, roiling from the flame's heat. When the food is nearly done, staffers pour kerosene on the fire, creating a flaming spectacle as the kettle boils over. Then, the feast begins.

Fish Creek also marks the entrance to Peninsula State Park, a 3,700-acre limestone headland that juts into Green Bay. Twenty miles of hiking trails crisscross the park, and there's even an 18-hole golf course.

Drive along the 8-mile Shore Road for a sampling of the park's many beaches, bays and campsites. You can tour the 125-year-old Eagle Bluff Lighthouse and climb the park's observation tower for views of the half-dozen islands just offshore. The hazy landscape you see in the distance is Michigan's Upper Peninsula.

Drive the Shore Road about 8 miles through the state park to its east exit, rejoining State-42.

-------- **4** --------
Ephraim
(Population: 260) Chances are, visitors who compare Door County to New England's Cape Cod have the village of Ephraim (pronounced EEF-rum) in mind. It's easy to understand why: Sailboats bob lazily in the harbor, homes and shops sprout up tidily from the hillside and twin white steeples stand tall against the blue summer sky. Since the 1850s, an unwritten law has dictated that all buildings be painted white or left as natural wood.

You'll see some of the prettiest views of this town from the water. Rent a paddle boat to explore Ephraim's gracefully curved waterfront. You also can arrange for a sailing trip around Horseshoe Island at the harbor's mouth.

Back on land, plan to visit the Anderson Barn Museum and dock. The area's first tourists arrived here by steamer at the turn of the century. Nearby, Wilson's Restaurant served

ice cream cones back then, just as it does today.

Drive 5 miles north on State-42.

-------- **5** --------
Sister Bay
(Population: 680) Sister Bay's most famous residents might well be the goats who munch on the thatched roof atop Al Johnson's Swedish Restaurant. The largest community north of Sturgeon Bay, the Sister Bay area always proves popular with shoppers. Galleries, displaying works of local artists and crafters, sprout up along State-42 and State-57. Those roads lead into the cozy downtown, where more shops await. Also, south 2 miles along State-42, test your miniature-golf skills in a large, parklike setting at Pirate's Cove.

Drive about 10 miles north on State-42, passing through Ellison Bay, en route to Gills Rock and Northport.

-------- **6** --------
"Top of the Thumb"
Few visitors can resist a trip to the tip of the peninsula (or "Top of the Thumb," as locals call it). From there, some vacationers travel by ferry to a pair of islands just off the mainland.

Gills Rock, a working fishing port, grew up at the edge of the peninsula. Nearby, at Northport, you can catch a car ferry to Washington Island, home of the nation's largest Icelandic settlement. The 4½-mile-long island is a fine place to experience the quieter side of Door County.

Cross Washington Island to reach Jackson Harbor and you can hop a smaller passenger ferry to Rock Island. The entire island is a forested state park, a great spot for hiking, fishing or picnicking.

Backtrack to Sister Bay on State-42 and drive 3 miles south on State-57. Then, drive 6 miles northeast on County-Q. Follow winding Cana Island Road for 2½ miles, until it ends at the causeway to the lighthouse.

-------- **7** --------
Cana Island Light
The trip from Sister Bay to Cana Island takes you through some of Door County's most diverse landscapes— from cherry orchards to birch forests to the acres of wetlands found along the

The landmark Cana Island lighthouse dates from 1869.

BUCK MILLER

shores of Mud Lake. When you reach the end of the road, weather conditions and wave heights will determine whether you can explore tiny Cana Island. Sometimes, you can walk to the island; other times, you wade. Still other times, you simply must enjoy the view from a distance.

Built in 1869, Cana Island lighthouse is on the National Register of Historic Places and open to visitors during daytime hours in summer.

Continue 4 miles southwest on County-Q to State-57, then drive 1 mile east on Ridge Road.

---------**8**---------

The Ridges Sanctuary

Ancient sand-dune ridges gave this 910-acre nature preserve its name. The unique topography has produced an outstanding variety of wildflowers, including 25 kinds of orchids.

You can learn more about the area on a naturalist-conducted tour or a self-guided hike. Afterwards, cap off your visit by relaxing at this lakeside preserve's excellent beach.

Backtrack to State-57 and follow it 8 miles south through the towns of Baileys Harbor and Jacksonport. Just past Jacksonport, turn left on Cave Point Road and follow it 3½ miles south to Cave Point County Park.

---------**9**---------

Cave Point/ Whitefish Dunes

Eons of pounding surf have transformed the limestone shore at Cave Point into a rugged, brooding landscape of jagged cliffs and deep caves.

Immediately south of Cave Point, Whitefish Dunes State Park extends from Lake Michigan inland to the shores of Clark Lake. The rarely crowded park harbors wetlands along a winding creek. Nearby stand the highest sand dunes in Wisconsin. Stay off the dunes to protect them, but you can enjoy the park's beach.

From the park, drive Clark Lake Road 4 miles west to State-57. Then, drive 10 miles south back to Sturgeon Bay to complete your tour. ■

By Tina Lassen.

A FLINT HILLS JOURNEY

Tall grass stretches as far as you can see in the Flint Hills of east-central Kansas, an area of prairie and rock knolls that extends roughly from Wichita north to Abilene and east to Emporia. Winds play across the nearly treeless landscape, creating swaying patterns of wheat and grass that extend for miles. The region, one of the last true prairies in North America, is a rare reminder of the time when open grasslands covered vast stretches in the middle of our continent.

Native Americans learned to survive in this unsheltered countryside. Today, Flint Hills ranchers still follow the ancient Indian custom of burning off their pastures. Flames often cast an eerie orange pallor in the skies. Rains transform the blackened landscape into multiple shades of green.

Towns that are steeped in Old West lore put out the welcome mat for visitors. Some of these communities, such as Council Grove, owe their origins to the historic Santa Fe and Chisholm trails, which once passed through the Flint Hills. Marshall "Wild Bill" Hickok kept an uneasy peace in Abilene, trail's end for countless cattle drives.

German-Russian Mennonites settled Hillsboro, and today sell their crafts and produce. Swedes migrated to Lindsborg and proudly keep their Old World traditions alive there.

Your 255-mile Flint Hills adventure begins and ends in Junction City, headquarters of Custer's Seventh Cavalry and less than 2 hours west of Kansas City. Along the way, the route circles through tidy towns of whitewashed wood-frame and stone homes. In between, the ever-present prairie spreads out before you. Open-range cattle, along with antelope and deer, graze on the tall grasses, while hawks soar like your escorts overhead.

Spring rains turn
the prairie into a
sea of green.

❶

Fort Riley

Just north of Junction City along US-77, Fort Riley's military traditions began in the days of the Old West. Soldiers from Custer's Seventh Cavalry first rode out from Fort Riley more than a century ago. The U.S. Cavalry Museum depicts the life of those elite horse soldiers. Many of western artist Frederick Remington's works are on display here, too, along with uniforms and weapons dating back to the American Revolution. You also can tour Custer's home, built in 1855.

Drive 2 miles south from Fort Riley to I-70. Drive 3 miles east to State-57, then 34 miles south through the rolling countryside.

❷

Council Grove

(Population: 2,230) A tree-shaded farm town, Council Grove claims a prominent place in American history. Hundreds of pioneer caravans rendezvoused in Council Grove before proceeding west on the perilous 550-mile journey along the legendary Santa Fe Trail. You can take a self-guided driving tour that includes 18 stops at historic sites.

The Last Chance Store (open for tours) sold sowbellies, beans and other supplies to those hitting the trail. Pioneers left letters for their friends beneath Post Office Oak, which is located downtown.

Council Oak Shrine commemorates another tree, site of an 1825 treaty signed with the Osage. The treaty ensured European settlers safe passage south. Custer owned 120 acres near yet another tree, known today as Custer Elm. The Kaw Mission State Historic Site once served as a school for Native American and white children.

Drive 21 miles south on State-57/177, through open farm country. The striking Z-Bar Ranch, the center-piece of the Tallgrass Prairie National Preserve, a new national park, over-looks the highway just before you reach Cottonwood Falls.

The Disney-esque Chase County Courthouse.

FRANK OBERLE

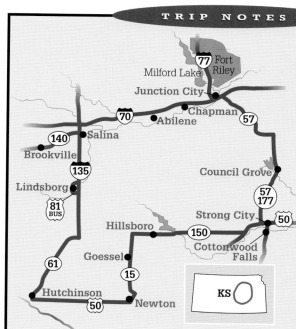

festival, in June **(800/732-9211)**. In Lindsborg, Messiah Festival of Music and Art, Easter week; Midsummer's Day Festival, folk arts and dancing, in June **(785/227-3706)**. In Hutchinson, the Kansas State Fair, in September **(316/662-3391)**.

SIDE TRIP—Drive 13 miles southwest of Salina on State-140 to the tiny town of Brookville and the historic Brookville Hotel, built in 1870 and furnished from the period. The hotel, now solely a restaurant, is known for chicken dinners **(785/225-6666)**.

INFORMATION—*Travel & Tourism Div., Kansas Dept. of Commerce & Housing, Ste. 1300, 700 S.W. Harrison, Topeka, KS 66603-3712 (800/252-6727); Abilene Convention & Visitors Bureau, Box 146, Abilene, KS 67410 (800/569-5915); Convention & Visitors Bureau of Council Grove, 200 W. Main, Council Grove, KS 66846 (800/732-9211); Greater Hutchinson/Reno County Convention & Visitors Bureau, 117 N. Walnut, Hutchinson, KS 67504-0519 (316/662-3391); Lindsborg Chamber of Commerce, Box 191, Lindsborg, KS 67456 (888/227-2227).*

TOUR ROUTE—About 255 miles amid the pastures, wheatfields and historic towns of east-central Kansas' Flint Hills region, including Mennonite and Swedish communities.

LODGINGS—Standard hotels and motels in Junction City, Abilene and Salina. Other choices: In Council Grove, The Cottage House, a comfortable, restored Victorian hotel (doubles from $58). In Lindsborg, the Swedish Country Inn, Swedish decor, as well as Swedish fare in the dining room (doubles from $49). In Chapman (15 miles east of Abilene), The Windmill Inn, a restored farmhouse with rocking chairs on its wrap-around front porch (doubles from $60).

CAMPING—In Lindsborg, Malm's Smoky Valley Plaza, landscaped with fishing ponds, also a restaurant. Along Milford Lake, northwest of Junction City. Council Grove Lake, northwest of Council Grove. Marion Lake, northeast of Hillsboro.

DINING—In Council Grove, the Hays House, established in 1857, and famous for fresh breads and Beulah's ham and grasshopper pie. In Lindsborg, The Swedish Crown Restaurant, for great Scandinavian dishes. In Newton, the Old Mill Restaurant, in a renovated flour mill. In Salina, The Cozy Inn, a six-stool eatery serving tiny hamburgers with fried onions the same way it has for 76 years. In Abilene, The Kirby House, fine dining in an 1880s mansion.

CELEBRATIONS—In Council Grove, Wah-Shun-Gah Days, inter-tribal powwow and local

---------❸---------
Cottonwood Falls

(*Population: 950*) Chase County's imposing French Renaissance-style courthouse—still used today—stands at the center of this prim, little town. The Roniger Memorial Museum, just behind the courthouse, is devoted to Indian artifacts and hunting trophies. The Chase County Historical Museum and Library chronicles the area's past.

But the best way to experience the history and lore of this region is on a self-guided driving tour that takes you through Cottonwood Falls' sister community, Strong City, immediately north, and along scenic backroads (get maps at the local tourism office in downtown Cottonwood Falls).

Drive 7 miles west of Strong City on US-50 to State-150 (which eventually merges with US-56) and continue 31 miles west to Hillsboro.

---------❹---------
Hillsboro

(*Population: 2,700*) With its busy downtown, Hillsboro resembles many other small Midwest communities, but it's in the heart of Mennonite country. The Adobe House Museum in City Park typifies the building style these immigrants of German descent adapted when they arrived via southern Russia more than 115 years ago. You also can view an enormous windmill replica.

Today, the compact farming community also is home to Tabor College, a Mennonite school and site of a historic Mennonite church.

Drive 6 miles west to State-15, then 8 miles south.

---------❺---------
Goessel

(*Population: 500*) A large, white, wood-frame church marks the outskirts of Goessel, another mostly Mennonite farming town. For generations, Mennonites have contributed to the Flint Hills. Their strong work ethic helped tame the frontier, and when they brought Turkey Red wheat to the plains from Russia, they turned Kansas into America's breadbasket. The Mennonite Heritage Museum tells their story.

Drive 20 miles south on State-15.

---------❻---------
Newton

(*Population: 16,700*) A regional farming center, Newton has long served as a hub for the Santa Fe Railroad. But away from the tracks, the town holds still more Mennonite history. A town founder, Bernhard Warkentin, brought Russian hard Turkey Red wheat to Kansas and influenced thousands of his fellow Mennonites to emigrate here. Tour the Warkentin family's 16-room Victorian mansion and the Old Mill Plaza the patriarch built. It's now the home of the Old Mill Restaurant.

The Newton Station, designed to resemble William Shakespeare's home, once was an important stop along the Santa Fe Railroad. Years ago, waitresses at the restaurant inside the station inspired the film *The Harvey Girls*, starring Judy Garland.

Wildflowers and 100 varieties of grass make up the living prairie that surrounds the Kauffman Museum on the Bethel College campus here.

Drive 33 miles west on US-50, past table-flat wheat fields.

---------❼---------
Hutchinson

(*Population: 39,310*) Some of the nation's largest grain elevators stand at the edge of this important Flint Hills commercial center. Location of the Kansas State Fair, Hutchinson also is known for aircraft manufacturing.

The bustling, small city boasts a unique attraction: The Kansas Cosmosphere and Space Center. The center features original NASA capsules marking every phase of America's space effort, spacesuits (the world's largest collection), a planetarium and Omnimax theater, plus many more exhibits. Kids arrive during summer to take part in the camplike Future Astronaut Training Program.

Drive 29 miles northeast on State-61 and 13 miles north on I-135. Take exit 72 and follow Business-81 for 4 miles into Lindsborg.

---------❽---------
Lindsborg

(*Population: 3,080*) Visitors from Scandinavia say Lindsborg looks "more Swedish than Sweden." You'll

In Lindsborg, the Swedish Country Inn's welcoming dining room.

ROY INMAN

find Old World-inspired shops, galleries, inns, bakeries and restaurants in the downtown, which resembles a European village. Browse the gift shop at the Swedish Country Inn for crystal, hand-knit sweaters and wool afghans imported from Sweden. The Birger Sandzen Memorial Gallery honors the prominent Scandinavian-American painter, with many of his and other artists' works on display.

You can learn more about Lindsborg's Swedish heritage at the Old Mill Museum, which also includes pioneer and Native American artifacts, a re-created pioneer town and the Swedish Pavilion from the 1904 St. Louis World's Fair.

Drive 4 miles east on US-Business 81 and 19 miles north on I-135, through Salina. Drive 24 miles east on I-70.

Abilene

(Population: 6,240) Chisholm Trail cowboys herding longhorns from Texas knew their work was done when they reached Abilene. Saloons, card parlors and dance halls greeted trail riders bent on celebrating—under the eye of lawman "Wild Bill" Hickok. You can glimpse the town's frontier beginnings at the Dickinson County Historical Museum's pioneer village.

When the cattle drives ended, Abilene was transformed into the quiet Midwest community that would mold Dwight D. Eisenhower, its most famous son. The former general and U.S. president's boyhood home is part of the Eisenhower Center, which includes the presidential library, museum and gravesite.

Grand homes line the main street into town. Two are open for tours: 110-year-old Lebold Mansion, with 23 rooms, and the ornate 1905 Seelye Mansion, with a ballroom and bowling alley. Also, save time for two of Abilene's most unusual museums: the Antique Doll Museum and the Greyhound Hall of Fame, celebrating the sleek racing dogs.

Follow I-70 about 20 miles east to Junction City to complete your tour. ■

By Ron Welch.

A RIVER VALLEY RAMBLE

The lazy "blue highway" that's the Ohio River rolls languidly along through southern Indiana, cutting a wending trail past nearly hidden towns and dense forests. Older and deeper by far than the Mississippi, the Ohio readily reveals its ageless spirit and long history to those who follow its course.

Abraham Lincoln's boyhood home lies near the river, along with Indiana's first capital, Corydon. Swiss settlers began new lives beside the river's banks, and their heritage lives on in the little town of Tell City. In Jeffersonville, still Indiana's boat-building center, a museum in a mansion that a shipyard owner's son built recalls the river's steamboat days.

Hoosier National Forest encompasses a vast, woodsy world all its own. Rocky promontories afford grand vistas of the river valley. Here and elsewhere, a labyrinth of limestone caverns tunnels beneath the bluffs. You can explore parts of that subterranean world at Wyandotte Caves and also at Squire Boone Caverns, which some say Daniel Boone and his brother discovered.

The river valley's character changes from rural to urban as you approach New Albany, just across the river from Louisville, Kentucky. The valley becomes rural again farther east en route to the town of Madison. There, you'll discover 133 blocks of 19th-century neighborhoods in nearly every architectural style popular at that time.

This Ohio River Valley adventure through southern Indiana follows the river's path along 200 miles of scenic roadways from Evansville to Madison. As you travel upstream beside the river's deep, steady currents, people and places with their own sense of time greet you around nearly every bend.

The *Delta Queen* cruises the Ohio, a river older and deeper than the Mississippi.

❶ Evansville

(Population: 126,290) Evansville curves along a horseshoe bend in the Ohio River, retaining the air of a busy river town from days gone by. As townspeople prospered from lumbering and furniture-making a century ago, they built ornate Victorian homes along historic First Street. Some now welcome visitors as bed and breakfasts and museums, such as the lavishly furnished Historic Reitz Home.

Also, visit the Museum of Arts and Science and the 67-acre Mesker Park Zoo, with its new primate exhibit.

Drive 7 miles south on US-41, across the Ohio River into Kentucky.

❷ John James Audubon State Park

This 482-acre state park, about a mile south of the Ohio River, is a bird-lover's mecca. The world's most celebrated avian artist's paintings hang in the Memorial Museum. The Nature Center, adjacent to the museum, houses bird exhibits, feeder stations and a viewing area that overlooks a small pond. Visitors come to camp, swim, fish and hike, too.

Backtrack to Indiana on US-41 and drive 4 miles northeast on I-164 to the Covert Avenue exit. Turn left (west) on Covert. Drive ¼ mile to the 4-way stop at Fuquay Road and turn left (south). Drive ½ mile to road's end at Pollack Avenue. Turn left (east) on Pollack and drive ½ mile.

❸ Angel Mounds State Historic Site

An interpretive center and exhibits explain the remains of a large community of prehistoric mound-building Indians who settled along the Ohio River from about 1250 to 1450 A.D.

Drive 4 miles east on Pollack Avenue to its end at State-662/66. Turn right and continue 20 miles, passing through the river town of Newburgh, location of the Newburgh Lock and Dam. Drive 15 miles north on US-231 to Gentryville (stopping at

Phil Jamison's Tell City Pretzels are hand-tied.

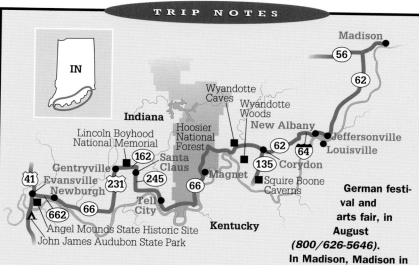

TOUR ROUTE—A winding 200 miles, following the Ohio River much of the way from Evansville to Madison.

LODGINGS—Major hotel and motel chains in Evansville and Louisville. Other choices: In New Albany, The Honeymoon Mansion, a bed and breakfast and wedding chapel along Mansion Row (doubles from $69). In Corydon, Kintner House Inn, an 1800s bed and breakfast (doubles from $39). In Madison, Stonefield's Dream Bed & Breakfast (doubles from $75).

CAMPING—Hoosier National Forest. Burdette Park and Audubon Park, near Evansville. Lincoln State Park, near Gentryville. Clifty Falls State Park, west of Madison.

DINING—In Leavenworth (10 miles west of Corydon along State-62), the Overlook Restaurant, reasonably priced home cooking, great river views. In

Starlight (7 miles northwest of New Albany), Joe Huber's Restaurant, down-home dining (try the fried chicken or honey ham). In Louisville, towboat Annie's, riverside views of Louisville's fountain. In Jeffersonville, Inn on Spring, fine dining in historic downtown area. In Madison, the Cinnamon Tearoom, country gourmet fare; The Wharf, casual dress and dining.

CELEBRATIONS—In Evansville, Ohio River Festival for the Arts, Mother's Day weekend (812/422-2111); Freedom Festival, hot-air balloon and hydroplane races, fireworks, late June–July Fourth (812/464-9576). In Henderson, Kentucky (10 miles south of Evansville), W.C. Handy Blues Festival, mid-June (502/826-3128). In Louisville, Kentucky Derby Festival, late April and early May, and the Kentucky Derby, first Saturday in May; Strassenfest/Artsfest,

German festival and arts fair, in August (800/626-5646). In Madison, Madison in Bloom, walking tour of prized gardens, end of April (812/265-2335); Madison Regatta and Indiana Governor's Cup, hydroplane races, early July (812/265-5000); Madison Chatauqua Fine Arts Festival, in late September.

INFORMATION—*Indiana Dept. of Tourism, One N. Capitol, Suite 700, Indianapolis, IN 46204 (800/759-9191); Evansville Convention & Visitors Bureau, 401 S.E. Riverside Dr., Evansville, IN 47713 (800/433-3025); Southern Indiana Convention & Tourism Bureau, 315 Southern Indiana Ave., Jeffersonville, IN 47130 (812/282-6654); Madison Area Convention & Visitors Bureau, 301 E. Main St., Madison, IN 47250 (800/559-2956); Louisville and Jefferson County Convention & Visitors Bureau, 400 S. First St., Louisville, KY 40202 (800/626-5646).*

the Antique Shak there). Drive 2½ miles east on State-162.

Lincoln Boyhood National Memorial

You can visit the farm where Abraham Lincoln lived from 1816 to 1830. Interpreters re-create the pioneer life he and other early settlers led. In summer, the musical drama *Young Abe Lincoln* plays at the amphitheater in adjacent Lincoln State Park. Nightly performances alternate with the musical *Big River,* based on *Huckleberry Finn.*

Drive 6 miles east on State-162 and south on State-245.

Santa Claus

(Population: 510) At Christmas, the post office in this town full of visitor attractions (including Holiday World theme park) hires extra help to handle letters shipped in from all over the nation to be mailed out with Santa Claus' cancellation stamp. Just off State-162, visit the Betsy Ross Doll House Museum, Toyland Museum and the Hall of Famous Americans, a wax museum.

Drive 8 miles south on State-245 to State-70. Turn left (east) and drive 2⅔ miles to rejoin State-66. Drive 8 miles east on State-66. Along the way, stop in Tell City for some of the Midwest's best pretzels. The Swiss-settled town is named for William Tell, the fabled Swiss folk hero.

Hoosier National Forest

Signs along park roads entice you to stop and explore trails, fishing holes and camping spots. But be sure to visit "Buzzard Roost," a breathtaking Ohio River overlook near the tiny park-encircled town of Magnet.

Drive east and north 36 miles on State-66 and continue east for 13 miles on State-62. Watch for signs that direct you to Wyandotte Woods and Wyandotte Caves, just off State-62.

Wyandotte Woods and Wyandotte Caves

Located in Harrison Crawford State Forest, this area attracts campers, hikers, horseback riders and other out-

door-lovers. You can take a guided tour through the limestone caverns.

Drive 10 miles east on State-62.

Corydon

(Population: 2,720) In this rural community with old-fashioned streetlights, you can tour the historic government buildings of Indiana's first state capital and visit the Battle of Corydon (Civil War) Memorial Park, just south of town along State-135.

Drive 12 miles south on State-135.

Squire Boone Caverns

A ¾-mile trail leads inside the caverns Daniel Boone and his younger brother, Squire, reputedly discovered in 1790. The nearby pioneer village features crafts demonstrations.

Backtrack to State-62 and drive 15 miles east. Drive 2 miles east on I-64.

New Albany

(Population: 37,400) Wealthy Ohio River merchants built regal mansions along Main Street, also called Mansion Row, in this modern city with a well-preserved past. Drawing on Victorian, Georgian and French Empire designs, the commanding 18th-century homes include the 1869 Culbertson Mansion (one of three homes open for tours). You also can tour the large atrium greenhouse at Abershold Florist along Silver Street.

Falls of the Ohio State Park, renowned for its fossil beds, is southeast of town along Riverside Drive.

From New Albany, drive 5 miles east on I-64.

Jeffersonville

(Population: 24,610) Jeffersonville got its name after town fathers laid out their city in a classic grid pattern that Thomas Jefferson devised. Some 119 buildings form a 10-block historic area on the riverfront. See exhibits that include displays of furnishings, boat models and photos at Howard Steamboat Museum, in an 1890s mansion along Market Street.

Jeffersonville takes its sports seriously. A manufacturing plant that wel-

Houseboats converge on Jeffersonville for a regatta each July.

comes visitors makes world-famous PowerBilt golf clubs.

Though this tour focuses on the Indiana side of the river, it's an easy hop across the Ohio to Louisville, Kentucky. Known for the Kentucky Derby, Louisville features theaters, shopping, galleries, fine dining and historic neighborhoods such as The Highlands and St. James Court.

From Spring Street in Jeffersonville, drive to 10th Street. Turn right (east) on 10th Street and rejoin State-62. Drive 37 miles north, then east, to State-56. Drive 8 miles east.

-------- **12** --------

Madison

(Population: 11,900) Madison looks more like a museum village than an actual town. Colonial spires and classic domes rise above tree-shaded parks and lawns. The town spreads out beside the Ohio River, surrounded by low, tree-covered hills. Conceived as Indiana's possible capital in 1809, city planners created extra-wide boulevards and parks with bubbling fountains.

The entire downtown—133 blocks in all—is listed on the National Register of Historic Places. You can explore neighborhoods lined with mansions built by traders who helped develop this once-thriving river port.

Timeworn stone walls and picket fences border the sidewalks, and lacy ironwork decorates homes and businesses. Visit the J.F.D. Lanier State Historic Site, one of several homes and buildings open for tours. Financier James Lanier constructed the mansion in 1844. His loans equipped the Hoosier army for the Union effort during the Civil War.

Madison also is known for its antiques shops, fine dining and bed-and-breakfast inns. Downtown, stop in eateries such as the Coffee Mill Cafe for delicious treats or the Broadway Antique Mall to browse 70 dealers (it's one of several antiques malls).

Clifty Falls State Park, where hiking trails lead to waterfalls and canyons, is 2½ miles west of town along State-56. ■

By Sara Corrigan.

BLUFF COUNTRY VISTAS

Though ancient glaciers flattened most of central Minnesota, the advancing ice wall somehow missed the state's southeast corner. It left undisturbed a landscape of soaring bluffs and deep, cool valleys, bounded on the east by the mighty Mississippi River, which runs wide and lazy even this far north.

This 200-mile bluff-country tour follows the Mississippi's course south from the historic river town of Red Wing, about 40 miles southeast of the Twin Cities. Then, it threads along beside limestone ridges that tower above the river. West of the Mississippi, green forests and farm fields cover the hills and valleys.

The route meanders through other history-rich communities, such as Lake City, Wabasha and Winona, that once prospered from the river's boat traffic. Today, they thrive on visitors who fill the 19th-century hotels, stores, antiques shops and friendly eateries that line their main streets.

At La Crescent, just north of the Iowa state line, orchards you can visit thrive on the blufftops, and apple stands dot the roadsides. The rocky soil makes fruit grown here especially flavorful. You travel inland through the Root River Valley, where an old railbed, transformed into a 35-mile paved trail for biking and hiking, parallels the highway. The trail carries you across bridges as it links villages along the Root River.

The little town of Lanesboro, at the valley's heart, hasn't changed much in a century. Time also seems to stand still in Harmony, the center of southeast Minnesota's Amish population. Cars share the road with black buggies here. In fact, thanks to the rugged terrain, much of this region remains in touch with times gone by. That's the true magic of Minnesota's bluff country.

Lanesboro, in the heart of the Root River Valley.

1 Red Wing

(Population: 15,130) Like the back of a giant elephant, 500-foot-high Barn Bluff looms above the business district in this old Mississippi River town.

Along the sidewalks stand restored brick buildings that sprang up when the town boomed as one of the world's largest wheat markets. Bright-colored flowers hang in pots from old-fashioned streetlamps.

Along Third Street downtown, the Mediterranean-style T.B. Sheldon Auditorium Theatre, recently restored to its 1913 grandeur, hosts popular performances year-round, as well as tours on Saturdays.

The St. James Hotel, a handsome, red-brick building trimmed in white, fills most of a city block along Main Street. Wheat barons built this landmark in 1875 to offer some of the poshest accommodations along the river. Sixty antique-filled guest rooms and the hotel's Port of Red Wing restaurant provide glimpses of that era.

From the hotel, you can wander a block north to Levee Park, a manicured green space and walkway that follows the river.

West of the business district, 19th-century homes line Red Wing's quiet residential streets. Many houses were styled to look as jaunty as old-time paddle wheelers, built with whimsical turrets and sweeping porches sporting "steamboat Gothic" trim. A number of these beauties, including the Pratt-Taber Inn, now welcome guests as bed and breakfasts.

Pottery- and shoe-making also helped put Red Wing on the map. On the edge of town, the cavernous factory that once produced Red Wing Pottery has been converted into an outlet mall, with more than 25 discount stores, and specialty and antiques shops.

Continue about 15 miles southeast on US-61.

2 Lake City

(Population: 4,400) A summer vacation mecca, Lake City edges the

L.A.R.K. Toy Factory owners Sarah and Donn Kreofsky with intricately carved figures for their old-time carousel.

PERRY STRUSE

Map labels: Red Wing, Lake City, Lake Pepin, Wabasha, Kellogg, Wisconsin, 61, Mississippi River, Winona, Minnesota, MN, Rushford, La Crescent, 16, Hokah, Fountain, 8, Lanesboro, Preston, 44, 52, Harmony, Spring Grove, Mabel

TOUR ROUTE— 200 miles, following the Mississippi and Root rivers, visiting orchards, recreation areas and history-rich towns.

LODGINGS—Standard motels in Red Wing and Winona. Other choices: In Red Wing, the St. James Hotel, a landmark with 60 antique-filled rooms (doubles from $115). In Winona, The Carriage House Bed & Breakfast, four elegant rooms in a grand old home (doubles from $70). In Lanesboro, Cady Hayes House Bed & Breakfast, a Victorian beauty with three guest rooms (doubles from $75); Mrs. B's Historic Lanesboro Inn & Restaurant, a pampering bed and breakfast along the main street (doubles from $50). In Preston, the Jail House Historic Inn, 12 rooms in a beautifully renovated 1869 jail (doubles from $69).

CAMPING—Great River Bluffs State Park (formerly O.L. Kipp) on a bluff overlooking the Mississippi, southeast of Winona. Sylvan Park, along the Root River in Lanesboro. In Preston, the Old Barn Resort.

DINING—In Red Wing, Liberty's Restaurant & Lounge for Mexican, Italian or American entrées served amid photos and other reminders of the city's past. In Wabasha, the Anderson House, old family recipes such as chicken and dumplings. In Lanesboro, Das Wurst Haus (open April 1–October 31), bratwurst, homemade root beer and fun; the White Front Cafe for breakfast and lunch, home-style cooking.

CELEBRATIONS—In Red Wing, River City Days, a food fair, parade, concerts, and an arts-and-crafts fair, the first full weekend in August (800/762-9516). In Winona, Steamboat Days, fireworks, carnival rides, fishing contests and art show, the week of July Fourth (800/657-4972). In La Crescent, Applefest, apple treats, orchard tours and carnival rides, the third weekend in September (800/926-9480).

INFORMATION—Minnesota Office of Tourism, 500 Metro Sq., 121 Seventh Place E., St. Paul, MN 55101 (800/657-3700); Red Wing Area Visitors & Convention Bureau, 418 Levee St., Red Wing, MN 55066 (800/498-3444); Lake City Area Chamber of Commerce, 212 S. Washington St., Box 150, Lake City, MN 55041 (800/369-4123); Wabasha Area Chamber of Commerce, Box 105, Wabasha, MN 55981 (800/565-4158); Winona Convention & Visitors Bureau, Box 870, Winona, MN 55987 (800/657-4972); Lanesboro Office of Tourism, Box 20A, Lanesboro, MN 55949 (800/944-2670); Historic Bluff Country, Box 609, 45 Center St. E., Harmony, MN 55939 (800/428-2030).

shoreline of Lake Pepin. The "lake" really is a 26-mile-long, 3-mile-wide stretch of the Mississippi River that's a favorite for all sorts of boating and for waterskiing, which was "invented" here in 1922.

You can rent pleasure craft at the Lake City Marina. One of the Mississippi's largest, it neighbors a 3-mile riverwalk, where stores sell crafts and other items. Stop at Pepin Heights Store on the south edge of town for fresh apples and sparkling cider.

Drive 14 miles southeast on US-61.

Wabasha

(Population: 2,500) Once a bustling river port, Wabasha has become so peaceful that eagles build their nests along the river—within the city limits.

Still, lots of summer travelers make weekend visits here, if only for the home-style meals at the Anderson House along Wabasha's main street. The restaurant is in a three-story brick hotel—Minnesota's oldest. Nearby, shops now occupy the town's restored early-1900s city hall.

Drive 5 miles southeast on US-61.

Kellogg

(Population: 420) At L.A.R.K. Antique Toys, fanciful creatures, each hand-carved and hand-painted, spin on a carousel that is a work of art. Take a ride and browse seven stores filled with playthings from handcrafted wooden toys to old-fashioned tin soldiers. Also, watch toy makers at work.

Drive another 31 miles southeast on US-61, following the Mississippi.

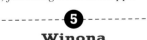

Winona

(Population: 25,400) Be on the lookout for Sugar Loaf, a hulking, 85-foot-tall chunk of limestone that crowns a bluff looming above the area's oldest and largest river town. The city, built on what once was an island, began as a rowdy stop for steamboats.

Named for a Dakotah Sioux princess, whose statue you'll find in a downtown park, Winona prospered from river traffic. Entrepreneurs built regal downtown buildings and homes.

Today, quiet enfolds the shady

streets. A bicycle path circles Lake Winona (actually the old river channel) on the south side of town.

Downtown, a walking tour takes you to more than two dozen structures listed on the National Register of Historic Places, including the 1857 Huff House. Exhibits trace the town's past at the Winona Armory Museum, one of the state's largest historical society museums.

At Levee Park, a walkway follows the levee, which is decorated with murals. The Julius C. Wilkie Steamboat Center in the park is a full-size riverboat replica you can tour, with steamboat models and other exhibits on the first deck and the Grande Salon on the second deck. The salon re-creates the romantic feeling of 19th-century riverboat travel. Follow Garvin Heights Road south from town to Garvin Heights for a blufftop view of the river valley.

Drive 22 miles southeast on US-61. Stop along the way to watch barges navigate Lock and Dam No. 7. You can try your luck fishing at the barge that's moored south of the lock.

La Crescent

(Population: 4,310) La Crescent sits on the Mississippi River bank opposite La Crosse, Wisconsin. You can rent boats at the town marina for fishing and sightseeing trips.

Locals proudly call their home "The Apple Capital of Minnesota." In town, several shops sell fresh fruit and apple treats. Twisting County-29, known as Apple Blossom Drive, climbs steeply to the ridge tops until you're almost 1,000 feet above the river. Some 800 acres of orchards cover the hills.

In spring, row after row of blossoms frame views of the Mississippi below. Stop at Leidel's Orchard and the Lautz Apple Market to buy fruit and for tours of their packing operations.

Drive 5 miles south on State-44 to Hokah and 23 miles west on State-16, leaving the Mississippi behind as you enter the Root River Valley.

Rushford

(Population: 1,490) Bicycle riders and other outdoor lovers flock to this 130-

Orchards cover
the bluffs above
the Mississippi
near La Crescent.

year-old village each summer to travel the 53-mile Root River Trail. The old railbed, paved for easy biking, hiking and rollerblading, begins at Rushford's restored depot. The trail roughly parallels State-16.

Portions of the trail also follow the same route Native Americans used for centuries as they traveled to South Dakota's Black Hills. Some area residents claim that you can see the ghosts of small bands, including young children and dogs, walking silently through the forests at night.

By day, the trail leads visitors over converted trestles and through tiny villages. At Peterson (6 miles west), the restored depot houses a museum. Whalan (13 miles southwest of Rushford) is where you'll find the Overland Inn. Following a hard day's ride, weekend bicyclists often stop here for the inn's renowned homemade pie.

Drive 18 miles southwest of Rushford on State-16.

Lanesboro

(Population: 860) The Root River Trail takes you right to the town's center. Nestled at the base of a 300-foot bluff, the entire business district of this picturesque town has won a spot on the National Register of Historic Places.

Lanesboro's two- and three-story brick storefronts line the wide main street. The buildings are legacies of a brief 1800s boom and the hard work of Irish, German and Scandinavian immigrants who settled here.

Shop at downtown crafts and antiques stores, including Down Home Antiques & Crafts, The Merchant of Lanesboro and Crown Trout Jewelers. At the Windy Mesa, you'll find southwestern crafts. You can browse and buy at a local winery. Watch cheese being made at a factory on the main street, which also sells the works of local Amish artisans.

Next to the trail entrance, you can explore a museum of local history. Bikes you can rent for a couple of hours or a whole day line up in front of Capron Hardware, just down the block.

For overnight stays, you'll find 20 bed and breakfasts in Lanesboro.

Drive 7 miles west on County-8.

Fountain

(Population: 330) The Root River Trail begins just east of this sleepy village. The Fillmore County History Center displays Native American and old military artifacts and clothing dating back to 1860.

Drive 4 miles south on US-52.

Preston

(Population: 1,530) In Forestville/Mystery Cave State Park, west of town along State-16, costumed park staffers give tours of an 1899 general store and its owner's home. Both once formed part of a town on this site.

Drive 12 miles east and then south on US-52.

Harmony

(Population: 1,080) Slow down! Horse-drawn buggies share the country roads as you approach this center for southeast Minnesota's Amish community. Downtown shops such as Michel's sell Amish-made furniture and crafts. More than 4,000 playthings fill the Harmony Toy Museum (open for tours). You can visit Niagara Cave, one of only two caves in Minnesota (south of town off State-44).

Drive 13 miles east on State-44.

Mabel

(Population: 750) Antique tractors and lots more vintage farm equipment fill the Steam Engine Museum in this quiet town, where Amish buggies sometimes roll along the main street.

Drive 8 miles east on State-44.

Spring Grove

(Population: 1,150) Decorative painting, known as rosemaling, adorns window boxes along the main street of this village, Minnesota's first Norwegian settlement. The Ballard House, a restored 1893 hotel, includes craft and antiques shops. The Bake Shoppe Cafe specializes in cinnamon rolls.

Drive 32 miles north and east on State-44, back to State-26 to finish your tour. ∎

By Barbara Briggs Morrow.

In Red Wing,
a trolley rolls past
the 19th-century
St. James Hotel.

DOWN-HOME OZARK ADVENTURES

The twisting, two-lane roads that wind through the age-old Ozark Mountains take you to the bright lights of Branson, Missouri—America's newest music and entertainment mecca. But they also transport you to the serene, scenic world of the Ozarks: steep hills where sheep and cattle graze; old river mills; broad, open lakes; and deep, green forests.

Visitors first came to southern Missouri's Ozark Mountain region, which stretches into Arkansas, at the turn of the century. Many were looking for the world Harold Bell Wright immortalized in his novel *Shepherd of the Hills*. The stage version of his work continues to play nightly beneath summer skies.

You'll discover homegrown artists and artisans here, hard at work on time-honored crafts in small towns such as Reeds Spring, Missouri, or gathered together at the Ozarks' best-known theme park, Silver Dollar City. You can travel along county roads to gristmills that grind flour as they have for ages, and visit down-home cafes that serve locally favored cornbread, barbecue and fresh-caught catfish.

Eureka Springs, Arkansas, a Victorian town brimming with antiques shops, old homes, and bed and breakfasts, nestles amid the Ozark Mountains in northwest Arkansas. Around giant Bull Shoals Lake, which stretches across both Missouri and Arkansas, you'll drive for miles following the lakeshore, which somehow has escaped 20th-century developers.

On this 270-mile loop tour, you can overnight close to the country-music excitement in Branson, settle in at Eureka Springs or choose one of scores of quiet lakeside resorts, where forested shore and water dominate your view. It's easy to see why visitors return to Ozark Mountain country year after year.

Kay Cloud
crafts dolls in
Reeds Spring.

--------- **1** ---------

Branson

(Population: 3,710) Located between Table Rock and Taneycomo lakes, Branson really is two towns in one: the old and the new. Turn east on State-76 to visit old Branson. You'll find the original downtown near the shore of riverlike Lake Taneycomo. More than 50 shops, many in buildings of rough Ozark stone, line old Branson's streets. A yesteryear dime store still serves a mostly local trade. The homey Branson Cafe fries up the legendary chicken dinners townspeople have savored for years. At the historic depot along East Main Street, visitors board glass-domed rail cars for rides into the surrounding hills.

The new Branson couldn't be more different. Today, it rivals Nashville, Tennessee, in country-music entertainment. To reach the new Branson, drive west on State-76. About 36 theaters line a 5-mile strip. Musical revues, featuring some of country-western's biggest stars, plus performers such as Andy Williams and Wayne Newton, glitter both day and night.

The strip includes water parks, miniature-golf courses and most of Branson's more than 75 restaurants, along with budget motels and pricey, new high-rise lodgings. Dozens of shops sell everything from souvenirs to fine crafts. An outlet mall that includes more than 50 discount stores marks the edge of town.

At best, expect stop-and-go traffic on the strip. To avoid the hubbub when approaching from the north on US-65, go west 2 miles on State-248, then south 4 miles on the Shepherd of the Hills Expressway, which brings you to State-76. The Visitor Information Center north of Branson (at US-65 and State-248) has area maps.

From Branson, drive 2 miles west on State-76.

--------- **2** ---------

Shepherd of the Hills Farm

Harold Bell Wright's frequent visits to this 160-acre homestead helped inspire

Branson, one of America's fastest-growing entertainment meccas.

SCOTT BONNER

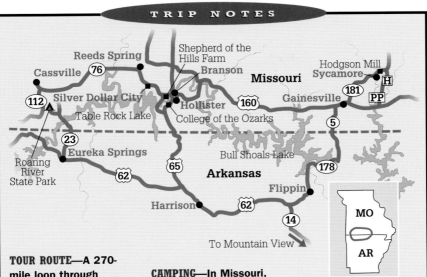

To Mountain View

MO
AR

TOUR ROUTE—A 270-mile loop through the scenic Ozark Mountains of southern Missouri and northern Arkansas.

LODGINGS—Branson claims more than 22,000 motel rooms. Resorts dot the shores of Table Rock Lake. Chain motels line US-62 on the outskirts of Eureka Springs; there also seems to be a bed and breakfast on almost every corner downtown. Try the plush Dairy Hollow House (doubles from $135) or the restored Palace Hotel (doubles from $127, no children).

Other choices: In Branson, the Palace Inn towers next to the popular Grand Palace Theater (doubles from $75); 12 miles south of Branson off US-65, Big Cedar Lodge, a first-class resort (doubles from $125). In the Indian Point resort area near Silver Dollar City along Table Rock Lake, The Tribesman Resort, kitchenettes and kids' programs (cottages for four from $60).

CAMPING—In Missouri, Table Rock State Park and Roaring River State Park. In Arkansas, Bull Shoals State Park.

DINING—In Branson, The Candlestick Inn, a beautiful hilltop view and great steaks; Dimitris Restaurant, fine dining along Lake Taneycomo. At the College of the Ozarks at Point Lookout (near Hollister), The Friendship Inn, down-home cooking. In Reeds Spring, Papouli's, casual atmosphere and Greek fare. In Eureka Springs, Bubba's, lip-smacking barbecue.

CELEBRATIONS—At Silver Dollar City, blue-grass and other music at the Great American Music Festival, 10 days in mid-May; National Festival of Craftsmen, early September through October (800/952-6626).

SIDE TRIP—Old-time Ozark crafts, customs and music flourish at the Ozark Folk Center

in Mountain View, Arkansas, about 60 miles southeast of Harrison (via State-14). At this 80-acre state park, you'll find 20 artisans plying crafts from broom-making to whittling. In the park auditorium, musicians perform generations-old tunes. The complex includes a 60-room lodge and a restaurant (501/269-3851).

INFORMATION—*Missouri Div. of Tourism, Truman State Office Bldg., Box 1055, Jefferson City, MO 65102 (573/751-4133); Branson Lakes Area Chamber of Commerce, Box 1897, Branson, MO 65615-1897 (417/334-4136); Arkansas Dept. of Parks and Tourism, 1 Capitol Mall, Little Rock, AR 72201 (800/NATURAL); Eureka Springs Chamber of Commerce, Tourism Information, Box 551, Eureka Springs, AR 72632 (501/253-8737).*

his turn-of-the-century novel about Ozark life. Costumed staffers re-create that era. Tour the homestead on foot or by tram. You also can ride to the top of 230-foot Inspiration Tower. Each summer evening, the author's story plays in an outdoor amphitheater.

Drive 3 miles west on State-76.

------- **3** -------

Silver Dollar City

Combine a friendly 1890s Ozarks town with country-music shows and restaurants, add some thrill rides and you've got Silver Dollar City, a family theme park. More than 100 crafters in old-time attire demonstrate skills that range from coppersmithing to basket weaving. Close by, squeals resound from visitors on the Thunderation roller coaster—one of more than a dozen rides. Restaurants serve country-style dinners and barbecue.

Drive 7 miles northwest on State-76.

------- **4** -------

Reeds Spring

(Population: 410) One by one, artists and crafters have set up shop in this tiny crossroads town. Pick up a guide to a half-dozen crafters' shops almost anywhere downtown. Be sure to stop at The Sawdust Doll to watch artist Kay Cloud at work.

Drive 1 mile south on State-13 and follow State-76 west as it twists along the ridge tops 33 miles to Cassville. Drive 5 miles south on State-112.

------- **5** -------

Roaring River State Park

The Roaring River in this 3,400-acre park provides some of Missouri's best trout fishing. You'll find picnic spots and campsites along the river. Hike 10 miles of trails (one goes to a waterfall).

Drive 5 miles east on County-F, then 18 miles south on State-86/County-P/State-23 into Arkansas.

------- **6** -------

Eureka Springs

(Population: 1,900) The hillsides in Eureka Springs are so steep, one seven-story hotel has a street-level entrance on every floor! The town first gained fame as a late-1800s health spa.

Five grand hotels from that era wel-

come guests today. Colorful Victorian homes, decorated with bric-a-brac, line narrow, winding streets that plunge sharply and crisscross every which way. Some 100 of these houses have been transformed into bed and breakfasts and tourist homes. Tour the 1880s Rosalie House, fancy as a wedding cake, with its gingerbread trim.

Visitors park their cars at their hotels or on city lots and board bright-green trolleys for tours around the historic downtown. Tucked shoulder to shoulder in buildings of native limestone, more than 150 stores tempt you with antiques, Ozark quilts and more.

East of town, a seven-story statue of Christ towers over the outdoor amphitheater that hosts *The Great Passion Play,* a world-renowned religious drama. West of town, the new Eureka Springs Botanical Gardens surround Blue Spring, a sparkling pool more than 500 feet deep.

Drive 36 miles east on US-62, through small towns such as Berryville and Green Forest, and 5 miles southeast on US-65/62. Fruit stands and antiques shops dot the roadsides along your way. Stop at the Tourist Information Center just northwest of Harrison.

------- **7** -------

Harrison

(Population: 9,920) Antiques shops pop up throughout Harrison. South of town, Dogpatch USA, a theme park based on the Al Capp comic strip "Li'l Abner," features kid-pleasing rides and a trout stream.

You have a choice here: Drive 35 miles north on US-65 back to Branson. Or you can continue 30 miles east on US-62, then head 10 miles north on State-178 at Flippin.

------- **8** -------

Bull Shoals Lake

Except for the resort town of Bull Shoals and farming communities such as Forsyth, Theodosia, Lakeview and Pontiac, you'll find very little development along the shores of this giant reservoir. Bull Shoals extends for more than 30 miles—from Arkansas all the way into southern Missouri. More than 1,000 miles of shoreline unfold north of the dam. To the south, the clear, cold White River meanders through

Eureka Springs, Arkansas, in the Ozark hills.

BOB BARRETT

forested hollows. At Bull Shoals State Park, you can rent boats or picnic overlooking the dam.

Drive 7 miles east on State-178, then 18 miles north on State-5. You'll pass a turn-off for Oakland, where small resorts cluster along Bull Shoals Lake at the Missouri state line. At US-160, drive 2 miles east to Gainesville.

Gainesville

(Population: 660) Early settlers built mills beside the region's springs and fast-moving streams. Several mills survive around Gainesville, the Ozark County seat. Stop at almost any of the town's businesses for a mill guide.

Drive 1 mile east on US-160, then 9 miles northeast on State-181.

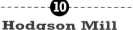

Hodgson Mill

Just beyond Sycamore, this 19th-century mill presides over a natural spring that powers its turbine. A gift shop inside the old mill sells fresh-ground flour and souvenirs. Nearby, a campground borders Bryant Creek, a favorite for inner-tube floats.

Drive State-181 north 5 miles to County-H. Drive about 5 miles south to County-PP, returning to US-160. Go 56 miles west on US-160, winding over ridges in Mark Twain National Forest. Drive 12 miles southwest on State-76. Turn south on Business-65.

Hollister

(Population: 2,630) English Tudor-style buildings line Downing Street. Drive Business-65 across US-65 to the College of the Ozarks, where students earn tuition at campus industries, including weaving, pottery-making, milling and baking fruitcakes you can buy. You also can tour a museum devoted to Ozark history and geology.

Drive about 1 mile south on County-V. Go 9 miles west on State-165, crossing Table Rock Dam (free tours) and passing Table Rock State Park (campsites and a marina with boat rentals) before returning to Branson. ∎

By Barbara Briggs Morrow.

LAKE MICHIGAN'S HARBOR HAVENS

L ake Michigan bestows cool breezes and mild tempera-
tures on the southwest corner of the Wolverine State.
Sleepy port towns line up along the lakeshore. Inland,
orchards and vineyards brighten the landscape.

A century ago, lake steamers brought crowds of vacationers
to harbor towns such as St. Joseph, South Haven and New Buffalo.
Cottages, grand homes and old-time resorts sprouted near the Red
Arrow Highway, which follows the shore.

Harbor country's first tourism boom ended when air travel
lured vacationers to far-flung destinations. Yet, after several
decades of benign neglect, the shore villages have sprung to
life again. Today, the old hotels and grand homes welcome
travelers once more as bed and breakfasts. Art galleries and
antiques shops dot the main streets, and pleasure craft crowd the
harbors. Dunes rise along the lake, and stretches of golden sand
entice strollers and swimmers.

Winding inland byways take you to more than 60 roadside
markets, you-pick farms, vineyards and wineries. Some wineries
welcome visitors with tours and special events. Farming centers
such as Dowagiac boast revitalized downtowns, where you can
browse shops and stop for lunch at homey cafes.

This 180-mile circle tour samples the best of harbor country,
from the lakeshore to rural landscapes. With so much to see and
do in this region, one visit won't be enough.

Catamarans
at Silver Beach
in St. Joseph.

❶ St. Joseph

(Population: 9,600) St. Joseph and its more industrial neighbor, Benton Harbor, straddle the mouth of the St. Joseph River. St. Joseph's downtown perches on a bluff, with sweeping lake views from every corner along its brick streets. The sleek, new Boulevard Inn towers just a couple of blocks from gingerbread-trimmed homes that 19th-century ship captains and lumber barons built. On Lake Boulevard, the street that runs along the blufftop, you can visit the Krasl Art Center and the Curious Kids Museum, with its hands-on art, history and science exhibits.

Crabapple trees and a century's worth of monuments dot the mile-long park along the bluff from the Maids of the Mist fountain to Pioneer Watch. This concrete platform stands on a spot that's been a lookout since 1670, when French traders erected Fort Miami nearby. Steep steps take you down from the bluff to Silver Beach. Swimmers and boaters crowd this popular, sandy stretch on hot summer days. Two 1,000-foot piers lead to a pair of lighthouses. Walk to the end of one of the piers in the evening, and you'll feel as if you've stepped into the sunset.
Drive 23 miles north on State-63.

❷ South Haven

(Population: 5,940) Pleasure boaters cruise along the shore toward the sheltered harbor at the mouth of the Black River. The harbor almost becomes a village of its own each summer. The historic Idler riverboat restaurant docks here, beside a new inn and a collection of shops perfect for browsing.

Across the harbor, the Michigan Maritime Museum traces the area's history from the Pottawatomi, who paddled the Black River in birchbark canoes, to the giant lake steamers that brought turn-of-the-century vacationers to South Haven. Stroll the 500-foot boardwalk that overlooks the harbor or stop for a picnic in the museum's

Bicyclists pedal the country roads around Three Oaks.

JOHN STRAUSS

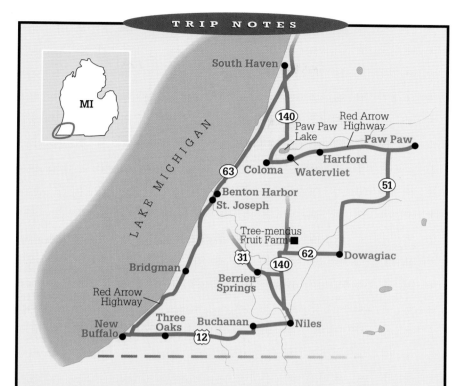

TOUR ROUTE—180 miles through resort towns along Lake Michigan's southeast shore, and through orchard and vineyard country inland.

LODGINGS—Standard motels cluster along I-94 near St. Joseph, on the outskirts of Benton Harbor. Other choices: In St. Joseph, the Boulevard Inn, plush, apartmentlike rooms (doubles from $99). In South Haven, the Carriage House, bed and breakfast in two Victorian homes (doubles from $95); the Old Harbor Inn, actually a new lakefront motel and shopping complex with spacious suites (doubles from $98). Just north of New Buffalo, The Inn at Union Pier, cheery rooms in a 1920s hotel (doubles from $125).

CAMPING—Warren Dunes State Park.

DINING—In St. Joseph, Schu's Grill, burgers and other casual fare, overlooking Lake Michigan. South of St. Joseph, Cafe Tosi, an area institution serving northern Italian cuisine. In South Haven, the Idler for fresh lake fish in a historic riverboat transformed into a restaurant. Near Berrien Springs, the Tabor Hill Winery for fine dining overlooking the vineyards. In Union Pier, Miller's Country House for rack of lamb and pasta.

CELEBRATIONS—In St. Joseph and surrounding towns, Blossomtime, the area's biggest festival and Michigan's oldest, a week of special events that include orchard tours and parades, in early May (616/926-7397). The Hartford Strawberry Festival, southeast of Paw Paw in Hartford, with parades, arts-and-crafts booths, a carnival and other events, 3 days in mid-June (616/621-4119). In Berrien Springs, the Berrien County Youth and Horse Fair, top show horses, a midway and agricultural exhibits, in mid-August (616/473-4251).

INFORMATION—*The Southwestern Michigan Tourist Council, 2300 Pipestone Rd., Benton Harbor, MI 49022 (616/925-6301). Harbor Country Chamber of Commerce, 3 W. Buffalo St., New Buffalo, MI 49117 (800/362-7251).*

waterfront park.

Drive south 12 miles on State-140 and 5½ miles southwest on Paw Paw Lake Road.

Coloma

(Population: 1,830) Coloma means "fragrant flower" in Spanish—a fitting name for this drowsy community surrounded by orchards. Miller Orchards sells cider and an array of apples in an 1800s peg-and-beam barn that owners Jim and Patty Miller restored.

Follow the Red Arrow Highway east through more fruit-growing communities. Refurbished storefronts, including shops selling antiques and model trains, line Main Street in Watervliet, 2 miles east. Roadside stands beckon from nearly every crossroads.

From Watervliet, drive 21 miles east on the Red Arrow Highway.

Paw Paw

(Population: 3,210) More than 90 percent of Michigan's grapes grow in the vineyards around Paw Paw. In the tasting room at the St. Julian Winery, the state's oldest and largest, you can sample some of the 36 wines that St. Julian makes and join a winery tour. Stop in the Apollo Wine Bar & Restaurant, filled with TV and other memorabilia.

Next door, Warner Vineyards occupies Paw Paw's renovated 1898 waterworks building. There, you can visit a champagne cave where bubbly ferments in classic French style. Take a self-guided tour that describes the champagne-making process.

The town of Paw Paw centers on a classic, clock-towered courthouse along the shores of Maple Lake. You can take a lake cruise on a pint-size paddle wheeler, *Princess Laura*.

Backtrack 4 miles west on the Red Arrow Highway and drive 21 miles south and west on State-51.

Dowagiac

(Population: 6,310) The Round Oak Stove Company put Dowagiac on the map during the late 1800s. Though the factory that made the stoves closed long ago, antique wood-burners stand in the windows of more than 20

restored stores along Front Street, the main thoroughfare. Join locals for coffee or genuine malteds at the Caruso Candy Kitchen. Mary "Butch" Myers dips chocolates by hand there, just as her father and grandfather did. Book lovers can't resist browsing stacks of vintage tomes at Olympia Books & Prints, also along Front Street.

Manufacturing and milling fortunes built the imposing homes along the surrounding streets. Follow a self-guided tour to beauties such as the 1893 stone mansion known as The Rockery and an 1858 Greek Revival that once belonged to one of Abraham Lincoln's aides.

Northwest of town along State-62, stop at Wicks' Apple House, a store and orchard three generations of the Wicks family operate. You'll enjoy the fresh fruit, gift shop and cheery cafe.

Drive 5 miles west on State-62 and 1 mile north on State-140. Drive 1½ miles east on Eureka Road.

Tree-mendus Fruit Farm

Herb Teichman's family established this sprawling orchard. Today, Herb says he spends almost as much time entertaining visitors as he does tending to the orchard's more than 300 fruit-tree varieties. You can drive the gravel lanes that wind through row upon row of fruit trees on your own or take a guided tour. Tree-mendus has hiking trails and wagon rides.

Backtrack to State-140 and drive 8 miles south. Then, drive 4 miles west on Pokagon Road to US-31.

Berrien Springs

(Population: 2,040) The columned 1839 courthouse on Berrien Springs' square looks as if it belongs in ancient Greece—not this friendly Midwest town. It's the only remaining county courthouse from that era in the state. East of town along Huckleberry Road, 5 miles of trails wind through the forests and marshes of Love Creek County Park.

About 5 miles west of town along Lemon Creek Road, sixth-generation vintner Jeff Lemon oversees wine-making at the Lemon Creek Winery and gladly shows visitors around. The

The end of a
typical summer
day in St. Joseph.

vineyard's classic barn stands near a tranquil pond. At Tabor Hill Winery, 5 miles west of town along Mount Tabor Road, you can tour the wine-making operation and dine at the restaurant overlooking the vineyards.

Drive 9 miles south on US-31, which becomes Business-31.

-------- **8** --------

Niles

(Population: 13,120) More than 300 years ago, a French priest founded a mission on the present site of this farming community. Fort St. Joseph Museum, behind City Hall along East Main Street (Business-31), houses French and Native American artifacts, as well as rare drawings rendered by Chief Sitting Bull while he was in a South Dakota prison.

At the Fernwood Nature Center, located 8 miles north of town along Range Line Road, trails lead through gardens and tallgrass prairie. The visitors center includes a fern conservatory and a tea room.

Follow the Niles-Buchanan Road about 5 miles west from downtown.

-------- **9** --------

Buchanan

(Population: 5,140) Along the banks of the St. Joseph, Buchanan calls itself "Redbud City." In spring, trees lining the streets explode with pink blossoms.

Buchanan's downtown merchants have restored their turn-of-the-century original brick shops and awnings. Stop at Palmisano's Cake House for a loaf of savory vegetable bread. Marz Sweet Shop, an old-time confectionery and soda fountain, hasn't changed in decades. Take home a selection of hand-dipped chocolates.

Pears Mill, an 1853 working gristmill, one of few remaining in the state, overlooks McCoy Creek. Located along Front Street, one block north of downtown, the mill opens for tours on weekends.

Drive the Redbud Trail 1 mile south to US-12. Drive 17 miles west.

-------- **10** --------

Three Oaks

(Population: 1,770) A cavernous factory that once made corset stays from turkey feathers looms over this sleepy town. But freewheeling optimism reigns at the Three Oaks Spokes Bicycle Club and Museum along Elm Street, home of the diehard local bike club. You can rent bikes there for pedaling the orchard-lined backroads.

Stop by the original century-old Drier's Butcher Shop along the main street for slow-smoked ham or fresh-made sausage. The shop ships meats nationwide.

Drive 5 miles west on US-12.

-------- **11** --------

New Buffalo

(Population: 2,820) In New Buffalo, condominiums rise along the harbor, now crowded with posh lake cruisers. Century-old Barbie's Department Store still anchors this prosperous resort area's downtown. Smaller shops also cater to visitors: an art gallery, antiques store and Country Mates, brimming with pottery, folk art and dried-flower arrangements.

Drive 13 miles north on the Red Arrow Highway. Bed and breakfasts, shops and galleries abound in the shore towns along this route, especially in Union Pier, Lakeside and Harbert. Plan plenty of time for stops.

-------- **12** --------

Bridgman

(Population: 2,140) High on a sand dune above Lake Michigan, Cook Energy Information Center presents free programs on how the adjacent nuclear power plant produces energy.

Two miles south of town off the Red Arrow Highway, dunes soar 240 feet above Michigan's longest public beach at Warren Dunes State Park. Climbers huff and puff to the top of the sand hills and then slip and slide back down. On clear days, hang gliders scramble to the top of Tower Hill, the tallest dune, and ride lake breezes. You can get information at this state park to explore the virgin forests at nearby 310-acre Warren Woods State Park.

Drive 10 miles north on the Red Arrow Highway to Business-94 and back to St. Joseph. If you can't make it by evening, be sure to find a spot along the way to watch the area's most spectacular show: the sun sinking slowly into the giant lake. ∎

By Barbara Briggs Morrow.

The Idler floating
restaurant at
South Haven
Harbor.

DISCOVERING RIVERBOAT TERRITORY

Traveling from Galena, Illinois, to Decorah, Iowa, you view some of the Mississippi River's most scenic stretches, before swinging inland through the rolling hills and farm country of the Upper Iowa River Valley. The glaciers bypassed this area where northeast Iowa and northwest Illinois converge, leaving hills and bluffs that some like to call "Little Switzerland." Green-and-white signs bearing a paddle wheel that marks the Great River Road guide you along part of this 120-mile route, unlocking the Mississippi's beauty and history.

Europeans first arrived in this area in 1673. By the early 1800s, river stops such as McGregor, Iowa, served as gateways to settling the region. Those towns retain a charm and atmosphere that belong more to the previous century than to today. Galena delights visitors with its Victorian-style homes, antiques shops and pampering bed and breakfasts. The city of Dubuque, Iowa's oldest, climbs up the hills from the Mississippi's banks like a miniature San Francisco—with a stately Victorian waterfront district and its own version of cable cars.

Ethnic traditions flourish in riverboat territory. Stone houses in Guttenberg, Iowa, reflect the town's German past. Decorah long has served as a New World mecca for Norwegian-Americans. Spillville, Iowa, a Czech settlement, helped inspire a renowned European composer's most famous work.

Besides the communities along this Galena-to-Decorah route, out-of-the-way stops between them also create lasting memories: the hidden creek that's a prime fishing hole, the little-known trail that leads to a rocky river overlook. All these secret and special places await on this weekend tour.

Galena, Illinois, the town that time forgot.

❶
Galena

(Population: 3,650) Lead mining brought prosperity to Galena. In its heyday, the town also was a fur-trading port and a stopover for steamboats that detoured east off the Mississippi for the short cruise up the Galena River.

Stately Civil War-era mansions and downtown buildings that the boom produced look much as they did 140 years ago. When the riverboat traffic ended, the town languished, and Galena remained—luckily, as it turned out—almost untouched for decades.

Lovingly preserved, Galena's vintage buildings now house restaurants, some 40 bed and breakfasts, and dozens of antiques and specialty shops. Along Main Street, shop at Banowetz for Victorian furniture and at Main Street Fine Books & Manuscripts for old books. Along Diagonal Street, visit the Galena Flatiron Building, two stories packed with antique pottery, prints, china, quilts and more.

Visitors create a festive atmosphere each weekend, filling the shops and restaurants. You also can tour Ulysses S. Grant's home, one of several historic buildings open to the public.

Drive 15 miles northwest on US-20, the Great River Road.

❷
Dubuque

(Population: 59,400) As your car heads toward Dubuque's bustling downtown, graceful steeples rise over blocks of venerable limestone and red-brick buildings. Elaborate mansions and houses trimmed in bric-a-brac cling to the surrounding hills and bluffs in this busy river port, which is Iowa's oldest city.

Look closely toward the river, and you'll see the slender arrow of the old brick shot tower. Here, hundreds of workers transformed lead into grapeshot during the Civil War, when Dubuque, much like Galena, prospered as a lead-mining center.

Today, Dubuque's riverfront bustles with visitors. Many come to shop or visit the Mississippi River museum

Decorah, Iowa, a town with deep Norwegian roots.

PERRY STRUSE

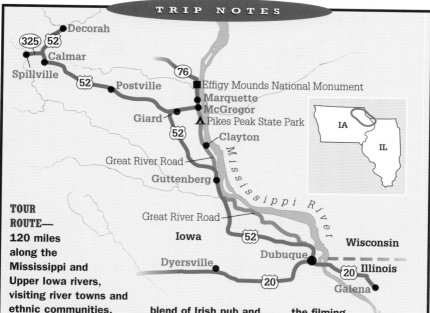

TOUR ROUTE— 120 miles along the Mississippi and Upper Iowa rivers, visiting river towns and ethnic communities.

LODGINGS—Standard motels in Dubuque. Other choices: In Galena, the DeSoto House Hotel, 55 rooms, Victorian decor (doubles from $99). Eagle Ridge Inn and Resort, south of Galena, homes/lodge rooms, great golf (doubles from $195, also packages). In Dubuque, The Hancock House, a restored mansion with a river view (doubles from $75). In Clayton, Claytonian Bed and Breakfast, river and bluff views (doubles from $60). In Spillville, The Old World Inn, where Dvořák stayed (Czech fare in the restaurant; doubles from $55).

CAMPING— South of McGregor, Pikes Peak State Park.

DINING—In Galena, Cafe Italia, for pastas, and, in the same building, Twisted Taco Cafe. In Dubuque, Pasta O'Shea's, a unique blend of Irish pub and Italian restaurant. West of McGregor (along US-18), White Springs Supper Club (try Ethel's barbecued ribs). In Marquette, The Captain's Reef, buffet and a river view at the Miss Marquette Casino. In Decorah, the Dayton House, in the Vesterheim Norwegian-American Museum, Norwegian specialties.

CELEBRATIONS—In Galena, Historic Home Tour, in June and September; Galena Arts Festival, in July *(800/ 747-9377)*. In Dubuque, Dragon Boat Festival/ Riverfest, colorful Chinese boats racing on the river, second weekend in September *(319/557-9200)*. In Decorah, Nordic Fest, crafts, costumes, food, last full weekend in July *(800/382-FEST)*.

SIDE TRIP—Fans of the movie *Field of Dreams* make pilgrimages to Dyersville, Iowa, site of the filming (25 miles west of Dubuque along US-20). Dyersville also boasts the National Farm Toy Museum and St. Francis Xavier Basilica, the only one of 33 basilicas in America in a rural area *(319/875-2311)*.

INFORMATION— *Galena/Jo Daviess County Convention & Visitors Bureau, 720 Park Ave., Galena, IL 61036 (800/747-9377); Tourism Office, Iowa Dept. of Economic Development, 200 E. Grand Ave., Des Moines, IA 50309 (515/281-3100); Dubuque Convention & Visitors Bureau, 770 Town Clock Plaza, Dubuque, IA 52001 (800/798-8844); Decorah Area Chamber of Commerce, 111 Winnebago St., Decorah, IA 52101 (319/ 382-3990); Eastern Iowa Tourism Assoc., Box 485, Vinton, IA 52349 (800/891-EITA).*

complex. You also can view Dubuque's Victorian architecture on horse-drawn carriage tours.

But the 116-year-old Fenelon Place Elevator (operating April—November 30) may provide the city's grandest view. Twin green-and-white cars rise nearly straight up to a hilltop residential neighborhood. At the elevator's base, you'll find the one-of-a-kind boutiques and crafts and antiques shops of Cable Car Square along Fourth and Bluff streets.

In the area of 13th and Iowa streets, a century of tradition lives on each Saturday during the growing season at the farmers market. There, produce vendors set up shop beside artisans and entertainers.

Drive 40 miles north on the Great River Road, passing through the tiny towns of Sherrill, Balltown, North Buena Vista and Millville.

--------- **3** ---------
Guttenberg
(Population: 2,430) As you head north, the Great River Road occasionally climbs away from the river, passing by cornfields and dairy farms, where Holsteins stand beside long milking barns. But the route always returns to the river. You get snapshot glimpses of the Mississippi as the road twists and dives among the trees.

The view opens, and the road straightens as you drive into Guttenberg. This mile-long town claims a dramatic site: The river rolls by on one side, and bluffs bound it on the other.

Street names such as Goethe and Schiller reflect the town's roots as a German settlement in the early 1800s. A self-guided tour leads you through Guttenberg's quiet, historic streets. Like most of the town's buildings, walls of the Old Brewery were built from native stone. The brewery has been transformed into an art gallery, bed and breakfast, and beer-and-wine garden. You also can tour its manmade limestone caves.

Stop by Kann Imports along River Park Drive. The gift shop stocks many unique items, such as hand-hammered Moroccan vases, as well as a large selection of Lalique crystal and Meissen porcelain.

When river barges approach town,

visitors rush for the tower at Lock and Dam No. 10 to watch the giant crafts pass through.

Drive 1 mile north on US-52 and about 15 miles north on the Great River Road, passing through Clayton.

--------- **4** ---------
Pikes Peak State Park
Farm fields immediately give way to forests as you follow the park road leading to Iowa's highest point above the Mississippi River, a bluff that affords a 20-mile, clear-day view. A paved bicycle trail that parallels the Great River Road links the park with Guttenberg.

Drive 2 miles north on State-340, the Great River Road.

--------- **5** ---------
McGregor
(Population: 950) Antiques shops, restaurants, and bed and breakfasts line McGregor's quiet Main Street. Jim Boeke's River Junction Trading Company stocks replicas of Old West gear and clothing so authentic that the shop draws clients from Disneyland and Hollywood studios. Main Street leads to the Mississippi River, where old boat frames create a nostalgic, postcardlike scene.

Drive 5 miles north on State-76, the Great River Road. Along the way, stop in Marquette at the Schoolhouse Mall, popular for antiques.

--------- **6** ---------
Effigy Mounds National Monument
Trails pierce the forest in nearby Effigy Mounds National Monument, leading to conical burial mounds and molded-earth effigies that resemble bears, deer and falcons. Overlooking the Mississippi, the 1,475-acre preserve includes 191 Native American burial mounds and a small museum.

Backtrack to Marquette and drive 9 miles west on US-18, through Giard, until US-18 merges with US-52. Continue another 32 miles west on US-52 (US-18 goes south at Postville). Drive 2 miles north on US-52 at Calmar and west 3 miles on State-325. The route takes you through the Upper Iowa River Valley. Bluffs and limestone palisades line parts of the river,

Ride in Dubuque's Fenelon Place Elevator.

PERRY STRUSE

but much of the valley unfolds like a single, serpentine cornfield.

Spillville

(Population: 390) The stone walls and spires of St. Wenceslaus Church greet you at Spillville. Czech composer Antonin Dvořák once played the church's pipe organ during daily mass. Dvořák visited this peaceful Czech settlement in 1893 to be among his countrymen. During that summer, he worked on his classic symphony *From the New World.*

The Bily Brothers Clock Exhibit now occupies the home where Dvořák and his family stayed. Frank and Joseph Bily spent years carving elaborate moving timepieces that are considered masterpieces of Old World craftsmanship. The brothers' carvings celebrate everything from Jesus' apostles and America's pioneers to Charles Lindbergh's transatlantic flight. The two brothers died within a year of each other in the early '60s, but the home remains open to visitors today.

Backtrack 3 miles on State-325 and go 7 miles north on US-52 to Decorah.

Decorah

(Population: 8,063) Limestone bluffs and forested hillsides frame the town Norwegian immigrants built in the 1850s. Locals proudly will direct you to the Vesterheim Norwegian-American Museum. There, you'll find carved furnishings, rosemaling, even a complete church with a steeple rising 65 feet. The museum gift shop sells Scandinavian books and crafts.

Downtown, Vanberia also specializes in Norwegian crafts, along with glassware and other imported items. The busy, compact downtown centers on a classic Midwest main street, a columned courthouse and historic buildings housing shops and businesses. Situated on top of a limestone bluff, Decorah's Luther College campus commands a sweeping view of the Upper Iowa River Valley and the surrounding woodlands. ■

By Rebecca Christian.

WONDERS OF THE NORTHLAND

Woods and water surround you as you travel through northeast Wisconsin's forests and along the Lake Superior shore of the Bayfield Peninsula. Green islands and craggy, sandstone cliffs rise to the north. Farther south and inland, small towns and cottage resorts interrupt the north-woods scenery.

From the community of Ashland, the largest in this region, south to Cable and Hayward, then back north toward the lakeshore, small towns and villages settled beside wild lakes and rivers reflect their fur-trading, lumbering and fishing heritage. Along tree-lined main streets, residents proudly direct you to the local historical museum and invite you to join in their tradition-rich festivals. Byways and highways lead into the woodsy wilderness of 860,000-acre Chequamegon National Forest.

As the route gently curves around the peninsula's Lake Superior shore, views are ever changing. You pass through postage-stamp-size towns with intriguing names such as Port Wing and Cornucopia. Take time to marvel at one of the sunsets that splashes pink and orange across the horizon.

At the peninsula's tip, the Apostle Islands, a national lakeshore, stretch out across the chilly waters of Lake Superior, just offshore from the town of Bayfield. Shops and restaurants greet vacationers in that picturesque town, which rolls down from the hills to the lake. It becomes a favorite of almost everyone who visits.

The gracious welcome you feel at Bayfield's bed-and-breakfast inns, among the finest anywhere in the Midwest, typifies the warm hospitality all along this 185-mile loop through the undiscovered northland of the Badger State.

The village of
La Pointe on
Madeline Island,
a boaters' haven.

❶ Ashland

(Population: 9,120) Ashland's Victorian-style brownstone buildings recall the days when this bustling, small city on Chequamegon Bay was a busy shipping and lumber center.

During the late 1800s, Ashland's gleaming-white Hotel Chequamegon ruled the lakefront social scene with chamber concerts, polite lawn croquet games and distinguished guests such as Mark Twain. Twice rising from the ashes, the hotel was completely rebuilt in 1986, featuring the same standard of decor and attentive service for which another former guest, John D. Rockefeller, would have tipped highly.

Today, beaches and parks line the bay. Pleasure craft bob in waters offshore. Prentice Park, on Ashland's west edge, is a 100-acre migrating stop and nesting grounds for waterfowl.

Visit Lake Superior Waterlogged Lumber, a firm that retrieves century-old lumber from the bottom of Lake Superior. Tours of the facility are available. The chamber of commerce supplies maps of area waterfalls.

Drive 9 miles west on US-2 and 14 miles south on US-63. Pine and hardwood forests line the roadways as you travel inland from Lake Superior.

❷ Grand View

(Population: 420) This historic logging town appears as a clearing in the forest. It's a community of square-front stores and modest, one-story homes where you can stop for picnic supplies, gas or lunch.

Drive 4 miles southwest on US-63.

❸ Chequamegon National Forest

Sioux and Chippewa once battled in the hills and ravines of this 860,000-acre north-woods preserve. Today, scenic drives crisscross the national forest. Four trail systems wind through its interior, including 60 miles of the North Country National Scenic Trail. You can access the trail along

Ashland's Hotel Chequamegon, rebuilt in 1986.

SUSAN GILMORE

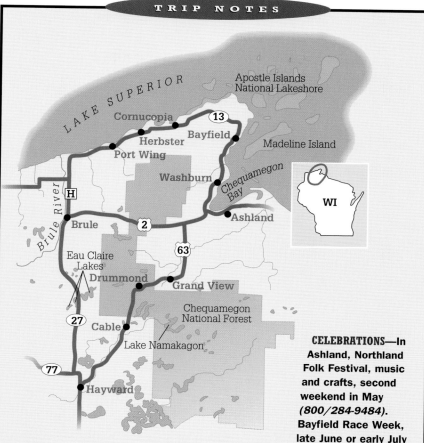

CELEBRATIONS—In Ashland, Northland Folk Festival, music and crafts, second weekend in May (800/284-9484). Bayfield Race Week, late June or early July (715/779-3335).

TOUR ROUTE—A 185-mile loop inland from Ashland and along the Bayfield Peninsula's Lake Superior shore.

LODGINGS—Standard motels in Ashland and Bayfield (reserve ahead, especially in summer). Other choices: In Ashland, Hotel Chequamegon, an imposing replica of a historic hotel (doubles from $85). In Cable, Telemark Lodge, resort amenities (doubles from $55). In Hayward, Best Western Northern Pines Inn, rooms with woodsy views (doubles from $49). In Bayfield, Old Rittenhouse Inn, Victorian decor (doubles from $99).

CAMPING—Chequamegon National Forest near Drummond (between Grand View and Cable) or east of Brule. Herbster's municipal campground along Lake Superior. On islands in the Apostle Islands National Lakeshore (check at lakeshore headquarters in Bayfield).

DINING—In Ashland, The Depot, a converted railway station. In Hayward, Chippewa Inn for hearty German and American fare. In Bayfield, Gruenke's, whitefish and whitefish liver specialties. In Cornucopia, Village Inn supper club. In Washburn, the Steak Pit for steaks and fish.

INFORMATION—Wisconsin Div. of Tourism, 2100 Beaser Ave., Ashland, WI 54806 (715/682-6529); Ashland Area Chamber of Commerce, 320 Fourth Ave. W., Ashland, WI 54806 (715/682-2500); Cable Area Chamber of Commerce, Box 217, Cable, WI 54821 (800/533-7454); Chequamegon National Forest, 1170 Fourth Ave. S., Park Falls, WI 54552 (715/762-2461). Apostle Islands National Lakeshore, Box 4, Rte. 1, Bayfield, WI 54814 (715/779-3397); Bayfield Chamber of Commerce, 42 S. Broad St., Bayfield, WI 54814 (715/779-3335).

US-63 near the town of Drummond.

You also can hike into two rarely visited, primitive areas within the forest at Porcupine and Rainbow lakes. Both areas are home to deer, bears, foxes and beavers. Chequamegon's many campsites (most fill up fast in summer) cluster around fishing lakes.

Continue 10 miles south on US-63.

Cable

(Population: 820) Cable's tiny business district anchors this summer recreation area. You'll find the region's prime attractions along backroads leading from the main highway. Warm water and fishing at Lake Namakagon (east of town off County-M) and at other area lakes lure visitors to lakeside cottage resorts, including Mogasheen and Ross' Teal Lake Lodge. Most lie hidden from the roadways, down forested lanes. At numerous public access points along the lakeshores, you can put in your own boat or simply enjoy the north-woods view.

Drive 17 miles south on US-63.

Hayward

(Population: 1,700) Small shops and restaurants line the main street of this busy resort town. Hayward supplies this region's quirkiest photo opportunity: a four-story muskie, mouth agape. The humongous fish is part of the National Fresh Water Fishing Hall of Fame, packed with fish stories, along with scrupulously compiled catch records and rare antique fishing gear.

In the summer, Hayward hums with vacationers. An old-time five-and-dime store shares the streets with candy shops, restaurants, clothing and souvenir stores, and miniature-golf courses. The area's lumbering history comes alive at the Logging Camp Museum, complete with lumberjacks and a re-created camp kitchen.

All year long, pristine woods and lakes lure nature-loving visitors to the Hayward area. The Namakagon River flows through town, and prime recreational lakes attract vacationers to the surrounding forests.

Drive 2 miles northwest from Hayward

on State-77. Then, drive 41 miles north at State-27. Halfway, you'll pass through the Eau Claire Chain of Lakes region, a 3,300-acre spring-fed chain.

Brule

(Population: 450) The Brule River, a great spot for canoeing or fishing, runs through this small town on its way north to Lake Superior. Stop and fish at turn-offs along State-27 going into town or County-H north of town.

Turn onto State-2 in the middle of Brule and stock up on bait, tackle and groceries along a ¾-mile strip of gas stations, stores and canoe liveries.

You can rent a canoe here and follow the river's northern course to Lake Superior. Signs of civilization soon disappear as you paddle your way through deep forests.

Drive 27 miles north and east on County-H/State-13. The location where the Brule River empties into Lake Superior is worth a photo stop.

Port Wing

(Population: 350) Wood-frame homes surround a small park in this little Lake Superior town. Follow the main street 1 mile north to the marina, with its cluster of charter fishing boats. Starting about 2 p.m. each day, commercial fishing boats head back to the docks, loaded with fresh-caught lake trout and whitefish.

Four miles east of Port Wing along State-13, a small park with picnic tables makes a great spot to watch freighters that ply Lake Superior. Stretches of sandy shore beg to be strolled. Perch on a favorite driftwood log to watch the sunset (after 9 p.m. in summer). The fiery, red ball descends slowly into the lake.

Drive 7 miles northeast on State-13.

Herbster

(Population: 80) Herbster includes a couple of taverns and restaurants, but lake views are what really draw visitors to this tiny community. You also can fish in the Cranberry River and drive the scenic Lenawee Rustic Road south of town.

Drive 8 miles east on State-13.

The National Fresh
Water Fishing
Hall of Fame in
Hayward.

--------- **9** ---------

Cornucopia

(Population: 100) Wisconsin's northernmost village affectionately calls itself "Corny." It's a one-general-store, one-gas-station kind of place, distinguished by its onion-domed St. Mary's Russian Orthodox Church. You'll discover quaint little shops in the harbor area. Nearby sandy beaches entice sunbathers and castle builders.

Continue 18 miles east, then 3 miles south on State-13.

--------- **10** ---------

Bayfield

(Population: 680) Shops and galleries cluster along the lakefront and the main street that leads from the docks of this small, New Englandlike town. Bayfield was built on hillsides that roll down to Lake Superior. Painters, potters and other artisans display their creations alongside boutiques, gift shops and fashionable clothing stores.

Up the hills overlooking Lake Superior's Apostle Islands, some of the Victorian mansions you see have been converted to bed and breakfasts. A wide porch wraps halfway around the 1892 Queen Anne-style Old Rittenhouse Inn, a vacationers' favorite.

Just 3 miles south of town along State-13, the Lake Superior Big Top Chautauqua plays all summer. Area residents perform dramatic musicals about local history. Sometimes called the "Carnegie Hall of tent shows," the chautauqua also stages concerts, comedy shows and light musicals.

--------- **11** ---------

Apostle Islands National Lakeshore

Cradled in Lake Superior's always-chilly waters, 21 of the 22 Apostle Islands and a narrow strip of the Bayfield Peninsula make up the Apostle Islands National Lakeshore. On the remote islands, green ridges and forests roll down to curving, solitary beaches. Forests for hiking and camping draw visitors ashore, where they also can explore ruins of old fishing camps and brownstone quarries.

Sailboaters favor this national lakeshore for its steady winds and protected waters. Lighthouses still stand watch on six of the islands. Rangers and volunteers lead lighthouse tours during the summer.

Along the shores of some of the islands, breezes echo through vaulted chambers and passageways of sea caves that kayakers love to explore. When the lake is calm, you're bound to see these craft around Devils Island.

The national lakeshore visitors center in Bayfield provides a good introduction to the area. The islands, which you can reach by charter boats and water taxis or your own craft, vary from more developed Stockton, with evening campfire programs, to wilder, primitive Outer Island.

Board the car-and-passenger ferry in Bayfield for the 2½-mile trip to Madeline Island.

--------- **12** ---------

Madeline Island

(Population: 180) The ferry from Bayfield takes just 15 minutes to reach the largest and best known of the Apostle Islands (not part of the national lakeshore). It docks at La Pointe, the 14-mile-long island's only town. You can stroll past wood-frame churches, old homes and restaurants. The Madeline Island Historical Museum recounts early fur-trading days.

Vans provide tours beyond La Pointe. You also can rent bikes and mopeds or drive your own car. Birdwatchers gather at 2,700-acre Big Bay State Park and Campgrounds. Big Bay Lagoon, which borders the park, draws canoeists and anglers. Landlubbers can test their mettle and enjoy gourmet fare at the 18-hole Madeline Island Golf Club and Clubhouse restaurant.

From Bayfield, drive 12 miles south on State-13.

--------- **13** ---------

Washburn

(Population: 2,800) Boat ramps and beaches dot the shoreline of this busy resort town, anchored on each end by parks that make great picnic spots. Learn about early logging families at a refurbished brownstone bank building that houses the Washburn Historical Museum and Cultural Center.

Drive 8 miles south on State-13 and 3 miles east on US-2 back to Ashland. ■

By Dixie Franklin.

Kayaking among
Wisconsin's
Apostle Islands.

ALONG THE WIDE MISSOURI

Meandering the two-lane highways and byways beside the coffee-colored Missouri River in southeast Nebraska, you'll discover a landscape of hills and river bluffs. Sleepy towns welcome you in green valleys beside the "Muddy Mo." Preserves and state parks along the way are devoted to nature and outdoor activities.

Omaha, Nebraska's largest city, makes a fitting starting point for your tour. The city grew up with the Missouri River. When Omaha became the eastern terminus of the transcontinental railroad more than a century ago, it linked the eastern U.S. with the far west. Today, modern office buildings rise near the riverbanks. The shopping, dining and sightseeing attractions here alone, including the trendy Old Market District, could more than fill your weekend.

South of Omaha, you'll encounter quiet river towns that echo the wide Missouri's frontier days. Once an important river port, Brownville settled into peaceful obscurity and remained virtually untouched for decades. Now, visitors come to gaze and browse along streets lined with 19th-century homes. In Nebraska City, where Arbor Day began 126 years ago, horse-drawn carriages ease along the lane to Arbor Lodge, a 52-room mansion you can tour at a historic park and arboretum.

St. Deroin, a living-history museum frontier settlement, is part of Indian Cave State Park, a rugged preserve. Across the river in Missouri, you can witness migrating waterfowl descending on Squaw Creek Wildlife Refuge in the spring and the fall.

Your 140-mile tour south along the Missouri River makes a leisurely 2-day drive that can begin with breakfast in a busy city and end with quiet sunset views of waterfowl.

Nebraska City's
historic show-
place: stately,
52-room
Arbor Lodge.

① Omaha

(Population: 335,800) Explorers Lewis and Clark stopped here on their voyage up the Missouri River. Later, fur traders established the Omaha area as a riverside outpost. When President Lincoln made Omaha the eastern starting point for the transcontinental railroad, the city boomed.

Signs along the Interstates direct you to Omaha's compact downtown near the Missouri River and to the Old Market District on the east side of downtown, just blocks from the river. A festive daily scene greets you in this area, which spans several city blocks. Street entertainers perform in front of restored warehouses filled with galleries, gourmet restaurants and antiques shops.

Try Antiques and Fine Arts along Howard Street for southwest-style, Mission and '50s-era antiques. You can walk east from there along Howard to Souq, a store that specializes in trendy clothes and jewelry.

Father Flanagan's historic Boys Town (it now accepts girls, too) lies west of Omaha off I-680. The self-contained community operates its own police and fire departments and schools, and welcomes visitors daily for self-guided tours.

South of downtown off I-80, the Henry Doorly Zoo received world attention when it opened its Lied Jungle exhibit. Animals, birds, fish and plants native to the world's great rain forests thrive amid waterfalls and lush foliage in the huge, indoor complex.

The zoo's most recent additions include a new IMAX theater, with a motion picture screen billed as the world's largest, and the $16 million Kingdom of the Seas, where you can walk, protected by a clear acrylic tube, through shark-infested waters.

Elsewhere at the zoo, you can view an aviary, giant aquatic animal pools and more than 2,000 species from the wild kingdom.

Omaha's other attractions include the Joslyn Art Museum, housing works by contemporary and Old World mas-

A church in tiny Brownville, a weekend haven for antiquing and summer theater.

P. DRICKEY

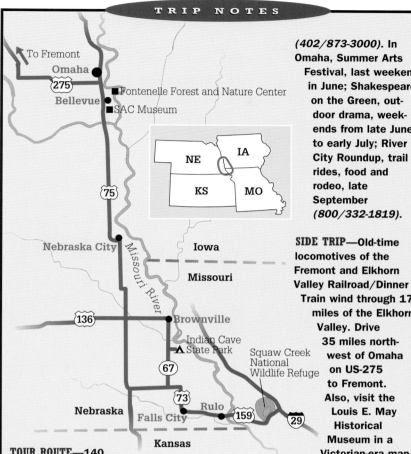

To Fremont
Omaha
275
Bellevue
■ Fontenelle Forest and Nature Center
■ SAC Museum

NE   IA
KS   MO

75

Nebraska City

Missouri River

Iowa
Missouri

136
Brownville
Indian Cave
▲ State Park
Squaw Creek National Wildlife Refuge
67
73   Rulo
Nebraska   Falls City   **159**   **29**
Kansas

(402/873-3000). In Omaha, Summer Arts Festival, last weekend in June; Shakespeare on the Green, outdoor drama, weekends from late June to early July; River City Roundup, trail rides, food and rodeo, late September (800/332-1819).

SIDE TRIP—Old-time locomotives of the Fremont and Elkhorn Valley Railroad/Dinner Train wind through 17 miles of the Elkhorn Valley. Drive 35 miles northwest of Omaha on US-275 to Fremont. Also, visit the Louis E. May Historical Museum in a Victorian-era mansion. *Dodge County Convention & Visitors Bureau, Box 182, Fremont, NE 68025 (800/727-8323).*

TOUR ROUTE—140 miles amid Nebraska's hills and bluffs beside the Missouri River.

LODGINGS—Standard motels in Omaha (the Westin Aquila is the premier hotel) and in Nebraska City. Also, in Nebraska City, Apple Inn, near attractions and shopping (doubles from $42); Lied Conference Center, resort with new lodge adjoining Arbor Day Farm (doubles from $80); Whispering Pines Bed and Breakfast, antiques, country atmosphere, near Arbor Lodge (doubles from $45). In Brownville, Thompson House Bed and Breakfast (doubles from $45).

CAMPING—Indian Cave State Park, south of Brownville.

DINING—In Omaha, Johnny's Cafe, great for steaks and barbecued short ribs; French Cafe, a gourmet bistro in the Old Market District; just south of downtown, Bohemian Cafe, European specialties, and Malara's, Italian cuisine. In Nebraska City, Ulbrick's Cafe, family-style fried chicken dinners. In Rulo, the Camp Rulo River Club.

CELEBRATIONS—In Nebraska City, Arbor Day Festival, parade, barbecue and games, last weekend in April

INFORMATION—*Nebraska Travel & Tourism, Dept. of Economic Development, Box 94666, Lincoln, NE 68509 (800/228-4307); Greater Omaha Convention & Visitors Bureau, 6800 Mercy Rd., Suite 202, Omaha, NE 68106 (800/332-1819); Nebraska City Convention & Visitors Bureau, 806 First Ave., Nebraska City, NE 68410 (800/514-9113); Missouri Div. of Tourism, Box 1055, Jefferson City, MO 65201 (800/877-1234).*

ters, as well as one of the world's best collections of western art. At the Omaha Children's Museum, kids can anchor a TV newscast or costume themselves to play adult career roles.

You also can visit the Great Plains Black History Museum and the recently reopened Western Heritage Museum in the renovated 1931 Union Pacific Railway Station. With its Art Deco grandeur restored, the museum houses the Union Pacific historical collection, including train cars, a re-created dining car and thousands of artifacts and photographs that trace the history of rail travel.

The Nebraska Furniture Mart and Borsheim's Jewelry are among the largest stores of their kind in the nation. And, if you love beef, don't leave town without stopping at some of the nation's best steakhouses.

From downtown Omaha, drive 13th Street about 2¼ miles south to the city limits, before it becomes US-75. Turn left onto Bellevue Boulevard and drive about ½ mile south.

--------- **2** ---------

Fontenelle Forest and Nature Center

Barely in the shadow of urban Omaha, Fontenelle Forest and Nature Center fronts the Missouri River. Hike through deep ravines along the riverbanks to ancient Native American earth lodges in the 1,300-acre forest.

Backtrack to US-75 and drive 39 miles south.

--------- **3** ---------

Nebraska City

(Population: 6,500) Nebraska City is a tidy town of wide streets and gracious homes that have 18th-century links to Missouri River traffic.

Visit John Brown's Cave, a short drive southeast. The humble cabin that sits atop the cave entrance hid runaway slaves on their way north to freedom along the Underground Railroad.

Few realize Arbor Day marks the birthday of Julius Sterling Morton, the Nebraska City man who conceived the only national holiday devoted to conservation. Morton and his wife, Caroline, began building the town's showplace, Arbor Lodge, in the mid-1850s. But their son, Joy, finished it. The

founder of Morton Salt Company, Joy had little time for his home here. For 2 decades, the Morton family used the 52-room lodge as a summer retreat.

Instead of selling it, Joy donated Arbor Lodge to the state to be preserved as a monument to his father. You can tour the classically styled mansion with its period furnishings. Then, stop by the orchard and gift shop across the road. In season, also plan to visit some of the area's other orchards.

The Lied Conference Center, a new log-and-stone lodge that is the centerpiece of a full-service resort, adjoins the farm and orchards. Trails for hiking and biking link the resort grounds and the farm.

Trolley-style buses shuttle visitors to all of Nebraska City's historic attractions, including the Old Freighter's Museum and Wildwood Period House, and the Factory Stores of America Outlet Mall. There, you'll find discount outlets for Bass Shoes, Jantzen Sportswear, Pendleton Woolens and other name-brand manufacturers. Stop, look and shop, then hop aboard another trolley to its next destination.

Drive 24 miles south on US-75 to US-136, then drive 10 miles east.

--------- **4** ---------

Brownville

(Population: 200) Nineteenth-century brick buildings make up this quiet community surrounded by hills. More than a century ago, heavy river traffic led many to believe Brownville would become Nebraska's state capital.

Instead, the village slumbered. Today, the entire town is listed on the National Register of Historic Places. Gift and antiques shops, as well as summer theater, have turned tiny Brownville into a popular weekend destination. Regional artists sell their works in galleries at the old schoolhouse. You can buy flour fresh-ground at the Brownville Mill.

Two excursion boats, the *Spirit of Brownville* and *The Belle* still cruise the river. And the Brownville Historical Society Museum recounts the town's colorful past. But to really learn the local lore, ask the locals themselves. You can hire Brownville's proud citizens—including the mayor—as tour guides.

Drive 1 mile west on US-136, then

The Old Market District in Omaha, with trendy shops and restaurants.

MIKE WHYE

9 miles south on State-67. Next, drive 5 miles east on State-S64E.

---------- **5** ----------

Indian Cave State Park

Ancient pictographs depicting animals and other natural scenes adorn the interior walls of Indian Cave, a short walk from the road. You can hike to the caves along a 20-mile trail system, with segments challenging enough to lure hearty weekend backpackers.

Horses for rent also take you to high points in this 3,000-acre park, among them St. Deroin, a re-created 1800s trading outpost, including a general store, school and ice house.

Backtrack on State-S64E to State-67, then go 8 miles south to US-73 and 9 miles east and south to Falls City. Go 10 miles east on US-159.

---------- **6** ----------

Rulo

(Population: 190) Not much more than a wide spot in the road, Rulo's real claim to fame is the 400-seat Camp Rulo River Club, a family-style restaurant with a river view that specializes in catfish and carp dinners for under $10. The restaurant's loyal clientele regularly doubles Rulo's population at dinnertime.

Continue 18 miles east on US-159, crossing the Missouri state line.

---------- **7** ----------

Squaw Creek National Wildlife Refuge

During migrating season, a half-million waterfowl stop over at this 7,178-acre wetland area on the Missouri side of the river. In spring and fall, migrating white pelicans, warblers and shore birds stop here.

The refuge is home to 303 species of birds. In addition to viewing exhibits, climbing the observation towers and hiking the trails, you can take a 10-mile auto tour, visiting bird nesting and feeding sites. You also may see some of the deer that populate the refuge.

Drive 2 miles east of the refuge to I-29, which travels back north toward Omaha along the Missouri and Iowa side of the broad river valley. ■

By Ron Welch.

LAKE HURON'S SUNRISE SHORE

un, sand, sea and serenity beckon all along Michigan's Lake Huron shore. You can claim a share of those lakeside pleasures when you follow the easy curve around the "thumb" of Michigan's Lower Peninsula, which resembles a giant's left-hand mitten.

Sweeping views of the deep-blue lake greet you along a route that leads through 19th-century lumber towns and fishing villages such as Bay City, Port Sanilac and Lexington. Many towns here have names that begin or end with "beach," "port" or "bay." Their quiet, tree-lined streets inevitably lead to marinas or breakwaters where pleasure boats bob on the gentle swell.

Nearby lighthouses beam warnings to ships offshore. Sunshine glistens golden on beaches and dunes, as everywhere, anglers swap fishing tales. In shore towns, neighborly residents, who welcome chances to chat, always seem to be celebrating something—from the Fourth of July to an ethnic festival or one of the nation's longest sailboat races.

The green-and-white signs that mark the Lake Huron Circle Tour Route guide you along a 140-mile northerly course (State-25) that links Port Huron, just above Detroit, with Bay City, along Saginaw Bay. When the highway swings inland, you pass tidy farms where orchards and fields of beans and sugar beets grow. Though parts of the route barely are beyond the shadows of Detroit, the city seems a million miles away.

Point Aux Barques lighthouse, near Port Austin.

---------- **1** ----------
Port Huron

(Population: 39,000) Giant ships pass almost close enough to touch as you stroll the walkway through downtown Port Huron, one of Michigan's oldest communities. The path follows the course of the Black River to where it joins with the St. Clair River. Pleasure craft and freighters ease through the St. Clair's wide channel, which links Lake Huron and Lake Erie via Lake St. Clair. Oceangoing vessels from all parts of the globe form part of the procession, along with sailboats, fishing craft and cruisers.

Near the mouth of the channel, Port Huron's famous Blue Water Bridge connects the U.S. with Sarnia, Ontario. Almost everyone crosses that span to make a brief visit to Canada.

But Port Huron, a former logging boomtown, probably is best known as Thomas Edison's boyhood home. The Museum of Arts and History preserves much of the inventor's memorabilia.

Drive 20 miles north on State-25.

Along the way, you'll pass through the little shore town of Lakeport.

---------- **2** ----------
Lexington

(Population: 770) Fruit pies help put Lexington, an old lakeside resort town with a small marina, on the map, and their ingredients are easy pickings at nearby fruit and berry farms. At Croswell Berry Farm, Rosalie Heufelder bakes up berry-berry-cherry pies (blackberries and raspberries mixed together with cherries).

Along Lexington's Huron Street, handsome Victorian buildings house antiques shops and boutiques that open onto brick sidewalks. Stop by the 125-year-old Lexington General Store, where bins of penny candy and everything from handmade linens to baskets crowds the shelves. There's also a 5-mile hiking and biking trail nearby. You can rent sailing and fishing boats along the lakeshore, and round out your visit with a stay in any of several cozy bed and breakfasts.

Drive 11 miles north on State-25.

The Seven Gables House in Huron City.

DENNIS COX

TOUR ROUTE—140 miles following the Lake Huron Highway around the easy curve of Michigan's "thumb," past beaches and old lumber towns.

LODGINGS—Standard motels are plentiful in Port Huron and Bay City. Other choices: In Port Huron, the Thomas Edison Inn for a river view amid posh surroundings almost under the Blue Water Bridge (doubles from $89). In Lexington, Britannia House, with a wraparound veranda beneath stout, old maple trees (doubles from $60). In Port Austin, The Garfield Inn, for a mansionlike setting (doubles from $75).

CAMPING—In Port Hope, Lighthouse County Park. In Port Austin, Port Crescent State Park. In Caseville, Albert E. Sleeper State Park. In Bay City, Bay City State Park.

DINING—In Port Huron, a view of the river and city at the Fogcutter Restaurant (the specialty: almond shrimp). In Port Austin, the Bank 1884 for elegant entrées and homemade desserts. In Bay City, the Lantern for dockside dining.

CELEBRATIONS—In Port Huron, Blue Water Festival, a 3-day Mardi Gras-style celebration that marks the start of the annual Port Huron-to-Mackinac Island Yacht Race, last week in July *(810/985-9623)*. In Bay Port, Bay Port Fish Sandwich Festival, in August *(800/35-THUMB)*. In Bay City, Bay City Fireworks Festival, 3 days of fireworks displays, a parade and other entertainment in Wenonah Park, around the Fourth of July weekend *(800/424-5114)*.

SIDE TRIP—Bavarian atmosphere reigns in Frankenmuth's restaurants, gift and craft shops, including Bronner's Christmas Wonderland, a year-round holiday store, the size of four football fields with thousands of ornaments and decorations from all over the world. Frankenmuth lies just 20 miles southeast of Bay City off State-15. *Frankenmuth Convention & Visitors Bureau, 635 S. Main St., Frankenmuth, MI 48734 (800/FUN-TOWN or 517/652-8666).*

INFORMATION—*St. Clair County Convention & Visitors Bureau, 520 Thomas Edison Pkwy., Port Huron, MI 48060 (800/852-4242); Huron County Tourism Bureau, 250 E. Huron Ave., Bad Axe, MI 48413 (800/35-THUMB); Bay Area Convention & Visitors Bureau, 901 Saginaw St., Bay City, MI 48708 (800/424-5114).*

The highway hugs the shoreline from Lexington to Huron City, with frequent scenic views overlooking Lake Huron.

Port Sanilac

(Population: 700) A snug, little harbor community with an old-fashioned brick lighthouse and a modern marina, Port Sanilac boasts 40 buildings more than a century old. Some house shops, while others serve as museums.

Costumed interpreters lead visitors through the 19th-century Loop-Harrison House. Within the cream-colored brick home, Dr. Joseph Loop's remedies still fill the shelves in his old-time medical office. You almost expect the lady of the house to descend the staircase in rustling taffeta and play tunes on the grand piano.

Drive 29 miles north on State-25. Towns en route to your next major stop are small. Along the way, you can view boats on the horizon and watch herring gulls floating on the breeze.

Harbor Beach

(Population: 2,000) The 1880 Harbor Beach Lighthouse stands guard over one of Michigan's largest manmade harbors. Bring along your clubs to play the challenging 18-hole Verona Hills Golf Course, 12 miles west of town along State-142.

Drive 8 miles north on State-25.

Port Hope

(Population: 300) Six miles north of Port Hope off State-25, Lighthouse County Park and the adjacent Thumb Area Great Lakes State Bottomland Preserve draw campers, swimmers, boaters and picnickers. Scuba divers explore offshore shipwrecks. Other visitors just read or lounge on the sand.

An 1857 lighthouse forms the centerpiece of Lighthouse County Park, where the lightkeeper's restored home serves as a maritime museum.

Drive 7 miles north on State-25.

Huron City

A living-history settlement, Huron City re-creates the life of an 1850s Great Lakes lumbering village with a general store, boardinghouse, church, museum and other buildings. The House of Seven Gables, with its white, wooden porch, high ceilings and gables, typifies the architecture found throughout the region.

Drive 3 miles west on State-25.

Grindstone City

(Population: 200) A century ago, residents of this aptly named town mined and shaped grindstones for grain mills. You still can see the giant milling stones, now used to decorate the yards of beachfront houses. In the evening, the park near the boat launch makes a great spot for watching the fishing fleet's daily return.

Drive 5 miles west on State-25.

Port Austin

(Population: 840) At first glance, Port Austin resembles a painting of a fishing village—too charming to be real. Wide, shady streets make the town ideal for exploring on foot.

Drop by the 1940s soda fountain in Finan's drugstore for a soda or chocolate Coke. Near the marina, the Captain's Quarters restaurant opens at 4 a.m. for anglers who leave port before sunrise. The big, round table in back is reserved for charter fishing captains.

Visit Port Austin's ½-mile breakwater during early morning or evening to watch the sun's twice-daily shows. Purple sunrises explode across Lake Huron, and sunsets splash blazing orange across Saginaw Bay.

From the tip of the "thumb" at Port Austin southwest to Bay City, sandy beaches and marshlands dominate the sheltered shoreline. From Port Austin southeast toward the open water, beaches give way to pebbled shoreline and rocky cliffs. Jade-colored breakers batter wave-worn cliffs. The rocky shore turns to bluffs, marked with turnouts for scenic views.

Drive 5 miles west on State-25.

Port Crescent State Park

Families splash in the gentle waves and bask in the sun along the 4 miles of

Dunes for bird-watching, sunning and exploring at Port Crescent State Park.

beach that front 565-acre Port Crescent State Park. The park was built at the site of a town abandoned in 1936.

Picnic decks sit atop a boardwalk that weaves among the dunes. Smoky aromas drift from busy grills beneath jack and white pines. The Huron Audubon Society maintains nesting sites for winged visitors—from bluebirds to ospreys—as well as birdwatching trails.

Drive 9 miles west on State-25. Contrasting with the rocky east side of the "thumb," the shore here is sandy, with low, grass-topped dunes along the lakefront.

Albert E. Sleeper State Park

Kids take flying leaps off 30-foot-high dunes and play tag with the surf at this 1,000-acre preserve of sunny beach and campsites.

Drive 5 miles southwest on State-25.

Caseville

(Population: 850) Head first for the busy harbor, where fishing boats cruise out toward deep water, while children feed the ducks and teens lounge on the grassy slopes. Restaurants and souvenir, craft and antiques shops line the town's main street.

Drive 8 miles southwest on State-25.

Bay Port/Sebewaing Area

Weather-worn commercial fishing boats tie up along the ruddy, wooden docks in the picturesque community of Bay Port *(population: 550)*. Residents tell you that the fish in Saginaw Bay are so big, "They catch the fishermen." In town, visit the Bay Port Fish Company to buy trout, salmon, perch and walleye. Then, continue along State-25 for 40 miles to Bay City.

On the way, you'll drive by cattail marshlands, home to waterfowl and other birds. Bird-watchers especially enjoy Wild Fowl Bay Wildlife Area, several thousand acres of islands and waters. (Visit the islands in your own boat; no public transportation.)

Beyond Pitchers Reef, you pass through the river town of Sebewaing *(population: 1,920)*, with its sugar-beet plant. The highway swings inland here. You're in farm country, and the scenery switches to flat fields, trim houses and barns. Roadside fruit and vegetable stands sell produce in season.

Continue 28 miles southwest on State-25 to Bay City.

Bay City

(Population: 39,600) Petunias nod like prim Victorian ladies in Easter bonnets along the streets that lead into downtown Bay City. The pastel parade is particularly fine along Center Avenue, lined with the palatial mansions of 19th-century lumber barons.

Bay City is Michigan's second-busiest port (after Detroit). Watch the procession of pleasure craft and ocean-going freighters from the Riverwalk, a 2½-mile hiking and biking trail along the Saginaw River's west bank.

Bay City's Avenue of the Flags leads to Wenonah Park. With a cascading fountain and reflecting pool, it's another good spot for a picnic and ship-watching. Nearby, the new Delta College Planetarium & Learning Center takes you to the stars via the latest digital graphics.

A panoramic view unfolds from the stone bell tower of Old City Hall. Delve into local history nearby at the Historical Museum of Bay County, housed in a former meeting hall where the Bull Moose Party originated during Theodore Roosevelt's time.

Downtown, The St. Laurent Nut House, established in 1904, still serves peanuts the old-fashioned way: piping hot. And, at the Bay City Antiques Center, you'll discover a block-long antiques mall under one roof.

Drive 3 miles north on State-13.

Bay City State Recreation Area

In spring and fall, flocks of Canada geese descend on Saginaw Bay's Tobico Marsh, part of this 2,000-acre preserve. Thousands of human visitors come to view the honking spectacle.

Follow 7 miles of trails or climb the two 40-foot-high observation towers for grand views. ∎

By Dixie Franklin.

Pleasure craft at
the Port Sanilac
Lighthouse.

WHERE LINCOLN LIVES

As surveyor, soldier, storekeeper, lawyer and legislator, Abraham Lincoln traveled his home state from Chicago to Cairo. But wherever Lincoln went, he always returned to central Illinois. This is where the 16th president matured into manhood. When he left Springfield for Washington, D.C., the newly elected President Lincoln said, "To this place and to these people, I owe everything."

Today, Lincoln's legacy continues to live all across central Illinois. You'll find it in New Salem, a museum village that includes the timber-frame store where clerk Lincoln developed his reputation for fairness and hard work. In Springfield, Lincoln's shadow still graces the only home he ever bought, along with his stark law office and the Old State Capitol. Here, the skinny, beardless Lincoln stirred the nation with his famous "House Divided" speech. Lincoln was buried in this city as well, and you can visit his tomb.

The rich farmland around Springfield includes many Lincoln sites, known mostly to area residents: the town of Lincoln, named for the young lawyer who secured the city's charter from the state, and Charleston, where Lincoln's parents lived in a modest cabin and remain today, buried on the prairie. As a bonus, you travel through central Illinois' Amish country: small towns and peaceful rural landscapes where time moves at a horse-and-buggy pace.

Lincoln leaps from the history books to become your traveling companion on this easygoing 245-mile, figure-8-shaped tour. Begin in Petersburg and walk the same paths as the failing shopkeeper, drive the route he rode as a successful circuit lawyer, visit the sites of his greatest political speeches and stand before the monument where Lincoln is preserved for the ages.

The Old State Capitol in Springfield, site of Lincoln's "House Divided" speech.

------- **1** -------
Petersburg

(Population: 2,420) Long a crossroads town, Petersburg prospered when Lincoln knew it. Restored fine homes climb the hillsides along the Sangamon River. The Petersburg Peddlers, Stanis-Sayre Antiques and The Rose Cottage are among a dozen craft and antiques shops in town. Petersburg's other famous adopted son, poet Edgar Lee Masters, wrote the *Spoon River Anthology* in 1915. Masters lies in the Oakland Cemetery on Petersburg's south side, four graves away from Anne Rutledge, Lincoln's reputed lost true love. Masters wrote her epitaph.

Drive 2 miles south on State-97.

------- **2** -------
New Salem
State Historic Site

From 1831 to 1837, Lincoln worked in New Salem as a store clerk, soldier in the Black Hawk War, postmaster and surveyor. Failing at most jobs, he studied law and was elected to the state leg- islature from New Salem. The town declined soon after Lincoln left in 1837 and lay dormant until 1932, when efforts began to restore it. New Salem now lives again as an authentic 1830s village, where you'll meet costumed "townsfolk" going about their daily chores amid timbered houses, a tavern, stores and school.

Drive 13 miles south on State-97, then 5 miles east on State-125/97.

------- **3** -------
Springfield

(Population: 102,200) Illinois' capital pulses with life, from downtown gov- ernment buildings to outlying ethnic neighborhoods and Lincoln sites. You can walk to most of them. Park at the Old State Capitol or the Lincoln Home Visitors Center and pick up a map.

Start downtown at the Old State Capitol, where Lincoln delivered his famous 1858 "House Divided" speech. The Lincoln-Herndon Law Offices face the capitol. South Sixth Street also borders the Old Capitol Plaza and includes bookstores, antiques shops

Lincoln Log Cabin State Historic Site near Charleston.

HOPKINS ASSOCIATES

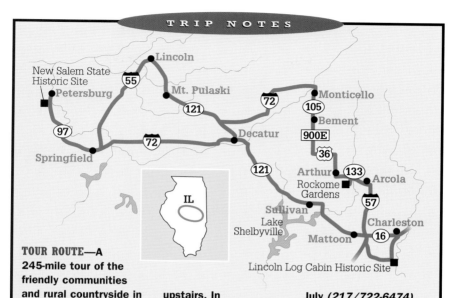

TOUR ROUTE—A 245-mile tour of the friendly communities and rural countryside in central Illinois.

LODGINGS—Standard motels in Springfield, Decatur, Charleston and Lincoln. Other choices: In Petersburg, The Oaks, a Victorian bed and breakfast in a mansion (doubles from $70). In Arcola, The Flower Patch, a pale-pink, Victorian two-story (doubles from $53). In Findlay (near Lake Shelbyville), The Inn at Eagle Creek, a resort with golf course and other recreations (doubles from $105).

CAMPING—New Salem State Historic Site, New Salem. Eagle Creek State Park (at Lake Shelbyville), Findlay. Weldon Springs State Park, Clinton (north of Decatur).

DINING—Near New Salem, George Warburton's Food and Drink, specializing in locally raised pork. In Springfield, Maldaner's, informal eating downstairs and special occasions upstairs. In Decatur, Central Park West. In Dalton City (southeast of Decatur), Stoney's steakhouse. In Arcola, French dining at The French Embassy in a bowling alley (that's right; call for reservations). At Rockome Gardens, Rockome Family-Style Restaurant, hearty home cooking. In Arthur, the Dutch Oven Restaurant, a local favorite. In Lincoln, Blue Dog Inn for sandwiches made to order.

CELEBRATIONS—At New Salem State Historic Site, Summer Festival, in July; Morgan Horse Show and Prairie Tales Festival, in late July (217/632-4000). In Springfield, the International Carillon Festival, bell music everywhere, early June (800/545-7300). In Arcola, Broomcorn Festival, in September (217/268-4530). In Mattoon (southeast of Sullivan), Herb Fest, last Saturday in April; Bagelfest, the end of July (217/722-6474). In Arthur, Cheese Fest, Labor Day weekend (800/262-2482).

SIDE TRIP—Before Lincoln lobbied to move the Illinois capital to Springfield in 1839, the burgeoning city of Vandalia served as the seat of government. About 65 miles south of Decatur along US-51, you can visit the graceful old capitol building (618/283-1161).

INFORMATION— *Central Illinois Tourism Council, 629 E. Washington St., Springfield, IL 62701 (217/525-7980); Abraham Lincoln Tourism Bureau of Logan County, 303 S. Kickapoo, Lincoln, IL 62656 (217/732-8687); Decatur Area Convention & Visitors Bureau, 202 E. North St., Decatur, IL 62523 (800/331-4479); Springfield Convention & Visitors Bureau, 109 N. Seventh St., Springfield, IL 62701 (800/545-7300).*

and galleries focused on Lincoln.

You can visit the only home Lincoln owned, now beautifully restored (get passes for free admission at the visitors center). The home anchors a shady four-block historic district, Lincoln's old neighborhood, located three blocks southeast of the Old State Capitol. Lincoln's tomb lies in Oak Ridge Cemetery, 3 miles north. A bronze bust of Lincoln, which Mount Rushmore sculptor Gutzon Borglum created, stands at the entrance.

Drive 38 miles east on I-72.

Decatur

(Population: 88,900) Parks, a large recreational lake and a fine zoo ring Decatur, an agricultural center since Lincoln's time.

Lincoln made his first political speech in Decatur (marked by a statue along Main Street), and he was nominated for the presidency here at the Illinois Republican Convention.

Central Park hosts events throughout the year. Nearby is historic Merchant Street, lined with restaurants and shops such as Ann's Gifts Plus, Del's Popcorn and Franny's.

The Macon County Historical Museum Complex, near the airport on the city's east side, includes a prairie village with homes, shops, a school and the Lincoln log courthouse, where the lawyer argued his cases. Nearby is Scovill Park, where you'll find a zoo and the Children's Museum of Illinois, both favorites with younger visitors.

Drive about 25 miles southeast on State-121.

Sullivan

(Population: 4,530) This small farming community brings nationally recognized actors to town each summer to perform at The Little Theater on the Square. Sidewalks around the square note each star's visit. The square also houses shops selling antiques and the Sullivan Bakery.

Drive 17 miles east and south on State-121, passing near 11,000-acre Lake Shelbyville with its marinas, campsites, inn and golf course. West of Mattoon, State-121 veers into State-16. Drive 12 miles east on State-16.

Charleston

(Population: 19,390) Home to Eastern Illinois University, Charleston has a relaxed, cultured, college-town air. Lincoln's father, Tom, and stepmother, Sarah, homesteaded south of Charleston. Follow Fourth Street, near campus, south 8 miles on well-marked county roads to the Lincoln Log Cabin Historic Site, where interpreters portray the Lincolns and their neighbors. Another well-marked route north from this farmstead leads to Shiloh Cemetery, gravesite of Civil War dead and Lincoln's parents.

From the cemetery, drive 5 miles north on the Lerna Blacktop Road to State-16. Drive west about 1 mile on State-16 to I-57. Drive north 13 miles on I-57 and 1 mile west on State-133.

Arcola

(Population: 2,710) An Amish farming town with I-57 on its east flank, Arcola caters to visitors. In the mostly brick downtown, shops such as Arcola Emporium and Rockome Store sell Amish quilts, furniture, foods and crafts.

Drive 4 miles west on Springfield Road. Watch for black Amish buggies.

Rockome Gardens

Amid peaceful rural countryside, visitors throng to this farm village that recreates 19th-century prairie life (check for special events April–October).

Drive 1 mile north on Rockome Road to Chesterville and 5 miles west on State-133.

Arthur

(Population: 2,120) You'll probably see Amish buggies along Vine Street, where shops sell locally made merchandise. The Pewter Spoon specializes in collectibles, and Calico Workshop stocks handmade quilts and Amish dolls. At the visitors center (Vine and Progress streets), pick up a self-guided tour map pinpointing the locations of some 40 Amish families who sell foods, furniture and crafts.

From Arthur, drive north on the Moultrie County Line Road nearly

Lincoln's parents' home, now a living-history museum south of Charleston.

5 miles to US-36. Drive 5½ miles west on US-36 to County-900E. Turn north and drive 9 miles on County-900E.

Bement

(Population: 1,770) Churches and a towering grain elevator anchor this classic central Illinois farm community. Bement also is home to the Bryant Cottage State Historic Site. Built in 1856 by Francis Bryant, this four-room cottage you can visit is where Lincoln met Stephen A. Douglas, a Bryant friend, to set the rules and schedule for their 1858 senatorial debates.

Drive 7 miles north on State-105.

----------⑪----------

Monticello

(Population 4,750) In this county-seat town, State-105 bisects Millionaires Row, where fortunes from selling patent medicines built grand palaces. View them on a walking tour of State and South Charter streets (get maps at the chamber of commerce office).

Continue on State-105 to I-72 and

drive 28 miles southwest to exit 35. Drive 17 miles northwest on State-121.

Mount Pulaski

(Population: 1,780) With its impressive homes along Main Street, this town has changed little since circuit lawyer Lincoln practiced at the Greek revival-style courthouse, now a state historic site.

Drive 11 miles north on State-121.

----------⑬----------

Lincoln

(Population: 16,330) Small shops front the courthouse in the only town named for Lincoln *before* he became president. Try Abe's Carmelcorn Shoppe along North Kickapoo Street for sweets or nearby Lincoln Antiques for collectibles. Lincoln College's Lincoln Museum displays artifacts and manuscripts. The rebuilt Postville Courthouse that circuit lawyer Lincoln practiced in is on the town's south side.

Drive 30 miles south on I-55 back to Springfield to complete your tour. ■

By Alan Guebert.

OHIO
RIVER
REVERIE

Follow the lazy Ohio River as it meanders past rolling, green hills and historic river towns. Along the way, you can join residents as they stroll beside the river levee, listening to the evensong of swooping bank swallows and lapping waves. Out on the river, paddle wheelers churn by, tooting their hellos to fellow travelers.

The river's tempo is slow—like a languid waltz. And the riverside highway from Marietta, the Northwest Territory's first city, to the town of Manchester, a little more than 200 miles southwest, puts you in touch with people and places that have their own easy sense of time. You'll see reminders of a long-past era when steamboats hauled coal and steel downstream, and floating palaces carried travelers in grandiose style. Today, you can climb aboard the *Becky Thatcher* showboat, permanently moored in Marietta as a restaurant and theater, or the *Valley Gem*, a stern-wheeler that Captain Jim Sands pilots out of Marietta, giving visitors a taste of the river's many moods.

Your 215-mile route leads to towns with tree-lined brick streets, hilltop mansions and fanciful wrought-iron fences. In between, the road curves with the river along towering sandstone cliffs and through vegetable truck farms tucked into deep valleys.

At roadside stands, neighborly farmers gladly share bits of local history. They might describe English or German ancestors who traveled by flatboat to settle the Ohio Valley when dense hardwood forests blanketed the region.

As night falls, red sunsets glint off the river, and you can hear loons skimming across the water. It's then that you'll discover what those who live along the river already know: The Ohio casts a timeless spell.

Riverboats still call at Ohio's first city, Marietta.

--------- **❶** ---------
Marietta

(Population: 16,500) Founded by 48 New Englanders in 1788, Marietta became Ohio's first city. Today, it graces the banks of the Ohio and Muskingum rivers like a lovingly tended garden. Wide, brick boulevards parallel the Muskingum River. Manicured lawns—the site of summer festivals—slope down to the Ohio, where the traffic of ferries, barges and pleasure craft lends the city a festive air. Like soldiers, grand old Victorian homes look out over Marietta from atop steep bluffs.

On warm summer evenings, residents of this gentle, little city eat ice cream cones along the river levee, where the historic Lafayette Hotel graciously presides over the scene. A century ago, paddle wheelers brought river travelers to the hotel's wide doors.

Captain Jim Sands' *Valley Gem* stern-wheeler departs regularly from Marietta, carrying visitors on river tours. Nearby, the *Becky Thatcher* showboat, permanently docked here, sparkles with strings of lights, inviting guests to dinner and an old-fashioned melodrama. The Ohio River Museum houses more steamboat-era lore.

In the historic riverfront district of brick- and stone-faced buildings along Front and Greene streets, you'll find antiques in The Old Tool Shop and gourmet noodles hanging up to dry in the Rossi Pasta Factory (take some home). A walking bridge across the Muskingum River leads you to more shops in historic Harmar Village.

Drive 12 miles southwest on State-7.

--------- **❷** ---------
Belpre

(Population: 7,190) At the Lee Middleton Original Doll Factory, you can watch as artisans make collector-quality dolls come to life. An outlet store sells the hand-painted dolls and accessories. Cross the river to Parkersburg, West Virginia, on the free bridge and catch the passenger ferry to Blennerhassett Island, a state park. It's a pretty picnic spot, and you can tour an Irish aristocrat's 1800s mansion.

Portsmouth's Boneyfiddle Historic District.

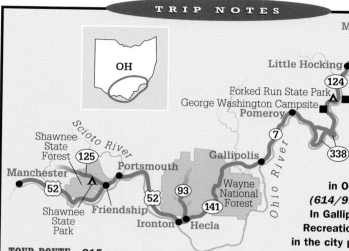

TOUR ROUTE—215 miles through the Ohio River Valley in southern Ohio, visiting historic river towns, scenic forest lands and peaceful farm country.

LODGINGS—Standard motels in Marietta, Gallipolis, Ironton and Portsmouth. Other choices: In Marietta, the Buckley House, with a river view from the bed and breakfast's porches (doubles from $70); the Larchmont, a southern-style mansion turned bed and breakfast in the historic district (doubles from $65); The Lafayette Hotel (doubles from $65); Clare-E Stern-Wheeler Bed & Breakfast (doubles from $70). In Pomeroy, the antique-filled Holly Hill Inn, one of the town's oldest homes, on a hilltop (doubles from $59). Near Portsmouth, Shawnee State Park Resort, 50 comfortable rooms in a stone-and-log building, with 25 nearby cabins (doubles from $86).

CAMPING—Forked Run State Park, near Reeds-ville. Vesuvius Recreation Area in Wayne National Forest, near Ironton. Shawnee State Park, near Portsmouth.

DINING—In Marietta, The Levee House Cafe, gourmet entrées in a charming, riverfront setting. In downtown Gallipolis, The Stowaway, a restaurant built underground. North of Gallipolis, the General Store Restaurant at Bob Evans Farm. In Ironton, C.R. Thomas' Old Place, grilled entrées in a family-pub atmosphere. In Portsmouth, the K&M restaurant for country-style cooking.

CELEBRATIONS—In Portsmouth, Appalachian Spring Festival, with clogging, arts and crafts, and storytelling, last week in April; Roy Rogers Festival, honoring the cowboy actor who grew up here and featuring memorabilia from Hollywood cowboy dramas, first weekend in June (614/353-7647). In Pomeroy, Big Bend Stern-Wheel Festival, first weekend in October (614/992-5005). In Gallipolis, River Recreation Festival, in the city park, around the Fourth of July (800/765-6482). North of Gallipolis, Bob Evans Farm Country Music Showdown, in June (614/245-5305). In Ironton, Tri-State Fair & Regatta, a 4-day riverfront celebration, last week in June (614/532-7980). In Marietta, Ohio River Stern-Wheel Festival, in early September (800/288-2577).

INFORMATION—Marietta Tourist & Convention Bureau, 316 Third St., Marietta, OH 45750 (800/288-2577); Meigs County Chamber of Commerce, 238 E. Second St., Pomeroy, OH 45769 (614/992-5005); Ohio Valley Visitors Center, 45 State St., Gallipolis, OH 45631 (800/765-6482); Greater Lawrence County Area Convention & Visitors Bureau, Box 488, South Point, OH 45680 (614/894-3838); Portsmouth Convention & Visitors Bureau, Box 509, Portsmouth, OH 45663 (614/353-7647).

Backtrack to State-7 and drive 8 miles south and west to State-124.

--------- ❸ ---------
Little Hocking
(Population: 800) In this tiny town—barely more than a wide spot in the road—you can buy seedlings, view model trains and get a jump on the holidays at Stahl's Nursery and Christmas Shop. The Stahl family has operated the business for more than 34 years.

Drive 11 miles south and west on State-124, a twisting, riverside route that passes through the small towns of Hockingport and Reedsville.

--------- ❹ ---------
Belleville Locks and Dam
From observation decks, watch long tows of barges pass through the Army Corps of Engineers locks and dam.

Drive 2½ miles south on State-124.

--------- ❺ ---------
Forked Run State Park
Fishermen reel in bluegill, catfish and striped bass at Forked Run State Park's 102-acre lake. Paddle a canoe into coves, where beavers and shy blue herons make their homes. A canopy of tall oak and maple trees shades picnic tables and the park's 198 campsites.

Drive 4½ miles southwest on State-124, passing through a bend-in-the-road town known as Long Bottom.

--------- ❻ ---------
George Washington Campsite
In 1770, George Washington camped here while surveying the lands of the Ohio Company. His journals noted the beauty of the Ohio Valley. Nearby is the site of Ohio's only Civil War battle. Union forces intercepted Confederate troops that General John Morgan led as they tried to cross the Ohio near Buffington Island.

Drive 7 miles south on State-124. Continue along the river about 20 miles on State-338 before rejoining State-124. Drive 7 miles northwest.

--------- ❼ ---------
Pomeroy
(Population: 2,260) Sandwiched between a bend in the river and a 200-foot-tall sandstone cliff, this village, which has no cross streets, bustles by day. Tugboat engines roar and churn the water into a white froth. The smell of yeast drifts from the Sweet Greetings Bakery. Take a warm raspberry Danish across the street to benches by the boat landing and watch pleasure craft dock.

A walking tour of Pomeroy includes the white-pillared Meigs County Courthouse. It's set into a steep hillside, with ground-level entrances protruding from each of its three stories.

In the Meigs County Museum, you'll see the furnishings and gowns of early English and German settlers. These were industrious folks, whose businesses once shipped tons of Ohio River salt and coal downstream.

Along Front Street, delicate cornices decorate the facades of 1800s-era buildings. Wrought-iron railings wrap around second-story porches that look out on the river. At night, store lights splay a rainbow of color on the quiet water.

Drive 22 miles south on State-7.

--------- ❽ ---------
Gallipolis
(Population: 5,090) The "Old French City" of Gallipolis (pronounced Gal-a-po-LEES) serves as a doorway to centuries past. Wide, tree-lined streets roll by large, brick homes in this historic, riverside community. You can enter the early 1800s at Our House Museum, once a river inn where locals entertained General Lafayette.

A walk along First Avenue leads past the homes of early settlers, French Royalists fleeing the guillotine. Mindful of the river, these settlers built their homes to foil floods. Many placed their living quarters above stores and other businesses, following the European custom.

Today's residents gather for summer festivals at City Park, where an octagonal bandstand graces a broad lawn. Across the street, in the Lafayette Mall, the congenial store clerks encourage shoppers to take dresses home "on approval."

Bob Evans Farm and the noted Midwest sausage-maker's original restaurant lie just 15 miles northwest of downtown Gallipolis along US-35.

Ever-changing
colors and moods
along the Ohio.

Quarter horses in white-fenced pastures whinny a greeting to visitors, who explore the working farm's log-cabin village and barnyards. Children go on hay-wagon rides. Quilt and car shows top a long list of summer events at the farm. The farm's 2-day Paddle and Saddle package includes canoeing and a trail ride.

Bird lovers seek out the nearby Elizabeth L. Evans Waterfowl and Bird Sanctuary to view ducks and Canada geese.

From Gallipolis, drive 2 miles south on State-7. Then, drive inland 47 miles southwest on State-141 through Wayne National Forest, passing through the small towns of Cadmus, Waterloo, Wilgus, Aid and Hecla.

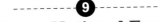

Wayne National Forest

Open fields mix with thick stands of hardwoods in the rolling hills of Wayne National Forest. Some 36 miles of hiking trails lead to dramatic rock ledges, lakes and lazy streams.

For an enjoyable short side trip: In Hecla, turn right at Howell's Hardware Store and drive to State-93. Turn right on State-93 and drive to Lake Vesuvius, site of an early iron furnace. The lake makes a fine swimming hole.

State-141 ends at US-52. Drive 1 mile northwest on US-52.

Ironton

(Population: 12,750) Brick Victorian mansions and ornate churches with Italian glass windows reflect Ironton's heyday during the pig-iron era. A stroll along Fifth and Sixth streets passes many of the homes that iron masters such as John Campbell built.

In pre-Civil War days, a tunnel guided fugitive slaves from the Ohio River to the cellar of Campbell's home, now the Lawrence County Area Community Action Organization.

Drive 28 miles northwest on US-52.

Portsmouth

(Population: 22,700) Wooded hills surround Portsmouth, a bustling river port. Cowboy actor Roy Rogers grew up in this small city where the Scioto and Ohio rivers meet. Murals stretch-

ing along the city's flood walls celebrate the area's past as a manufacturing center for steel and clay products.

In the Boneyfiddle Historic District, Portsmouth's original downtown, venerable storefronts reveal more than a dozen shops. The Leading Lady stocks a fine collection of china figurines.

Drive 8 miles southwest on US-52.

Shawnee State Park and Shawnee State Forest

Pick up forest maps at the state forest headquarters along US-52, 7 miles southwest of Portsmouth, for a scenic trip to Shawnee State Park. The state park is 5 miles west of the town of Friendship along State-125.

Ohio's largest state forest, 63,000-acre Shawnee, surrounds the state park. The forest's ridges take you more than 1,000 feet above the Ohio River Valley and overlook tranquil Turkey Creek Lake. Stay at Shawnee State Park Resort, a handsome new log-and-stone lodge, with a wide view of the lake and surrounding hills.

You can see for miles standing atop Picnic Point, just one of several turn-offs along the 35-mile Panorama Scenic Loop. Haze floats above the forested hills and hollows that descend to the river. Wear sturdy shoes for the 6½-mile trail that starts at the Turkey Creek Lake Nature Center.

Backtrack south on State-125 to US-52. Then, drive 34 miles west on US-52.

Manchester

(Population: 2,310) It's an easy drive to Manchester, past stone houses, vine-covered barns and lazy Holstein herds. Just west of town (2½ miles on US-52), grapes from vineyards of Moyer's Winery and Restaurant produce nine wines and a variety of champagnes, a reminder of years past when the region was famous for its vineyards.

Inland, just north of town, wild-flowers and herbs blanket the knobby hills. You can tour the fragrant gardens of Lewis Mountain Herbs & Everlastings. Sweet-smelling wreaths, dried flowers and potpourri also await at Hopewell Farms. ■

By Ellen Gerl.

Good times on the river: Marietta's annual Stern-Wheel Festival.

BROWN
COUNTY
BACKROADS

outh of Indianapolis, Indiana's flat farm country begins to dip and roll. Twisting two-lanes zigzag to ridge tops, where you can see for miles; then they plunge into mist-shrouded hollows. Much of Brown County, at the heart of this region, remains undeveloped, embracing woodsy wilderness and recreation areas that include Indiana's largest state park and part of vast Hoosier National Forest. West of the Brown County seat town of Nashville, Lake Monroe, Indiana's largest manmade reservoir, beckons boaters and anglers.

Because of the rugged terrain, only the hardiest pioneers settled here, and progress came slowly. At the turn of the century, the simple lifestyle and dramatic hill-country vistas began attracting an artists' colony that still flourishes here. In Nashville, crafters' and artisans' studios, art galleries and other shops fill cottages and log cabins along the main streets.

Outside town, roads travel through woods so thick that branches form canopies overhead and almost brush the sides of cars. These routes lead to hamlets with single-digit populations and whimsical names that beg explanation: Gnaw Bone, Bear Wallow and Pikes Peak (actually in one of the county's flatter areas). More than 500 log cabins still dot Brown County.

On the fringes of this hill-country region, you'll discover the bustling city of Bloomington (home of Indiana University) and Columbus, a unique showplace with more than 50 buildings that acclaimed architects have designed.

Even the state highways twist and turn as they meander through the hills, so be sure to allow plenty of time for this loop route of roughly 185 miles. Besides, no one hurries here; it's the Brown County way.

Vast forests and
timeworn hills,
60 miles south
of Indianapolis.

➊

Nashville

(Population: 870) Wooded hillsides frame Nashville's tree-lined streets. The shopping district centers on the intersection of Main and Van Buren streets. Throughout the town, you'll find turn-of-the-century buildings (old-time log cabins and clapboard homes), along with new storefronts designed to look as if they'd stood for generations.

The buildings house more than 300 craft and antiques shops. Many of Nashville's shops double as workplaces for the town's artisans—50, at last count. The Brown County Weavery, with its nubby, handmade shawls and ponchos in a rainbow of soft hues, fills a log cabin in a peaceful grove. Andy Huddleston, a potter, works in a white cottage set back from the sidewalk. He lines up his plates, bowls and candle holders for sale out front.

The Brown County Craft Gallery on Main Street displays and sells the works of two dozen local crafters—from quilts and pottery to handmade jewelry and baskets.

Many of the other artists who live and work in Brown County display their creations at the Brown County Art Gallery, as well as at the Brown County Art Guild. Forested landscapes share the walls with bright, contemporary paintings. You can watch artists work at the gallery at least a couple of days each week.

Around midday in Nashville, aromas waft from restaurants tucked amid the shops. You can savor an old-fashioned Sunday dinner any day of the week at eateries such as the Nashville House, a restaurant that's as cozy as a farmhouse kitchen with its stone fireplace and red-and-white-checked tablecloths. Be sure to try the fried biscuits.

Drive 2 miles southwest on State-46.

➋

Brown County State Park

Follow the winding blacktops as they climb through Indiana's largest and

Artist Kaye Pool at her home studio in Nashville.

MICHAEL VAUGHN

inventive cuisine; Little Zagreb's for juicy steaks and ribs. In Columbus, Zaharako's, thick malts and sandwiches in a classic soda-fountain setting. In Story, The Story Inn, antique-filled dining room in a restored general store (also a bed and breakfast).

CELEBRATIONS—The Nashville area Log Cabin Tour, visits to several restored Brown County log cabins, in late May (800/753-3255). In Bloomington, Taste of Bloomington, fare from 30 city restaurants, plus entertainment, usually the second weekend in June; Lotus World Music and Arts Festival, food and music from different countries (800/800-0037).

INFORMATION—*Indiana Dept. of Commerce, Tourism Development Div., 1 N. Capitol, Suite 700, Indianapolis, IN 46204 (800/759-9191); Brown County Convention & Visitors Bureau, Box 840, Nashville, IN 47448 (800/753-3255); Bloomington/Monroe County Convention & Visitors Bureau, 2855 N. Walnut St., Bloomington, IN 47404 (800/800-0037); Columbus Area Visitor Center, 506 Fifth St., Columbus, IN 47201 (812/378-2622).*

TOUR ROUTE—About 185 miles through the heart of southern Indiana's hill country, visiting neighborly towns, scenic parks and forests, with a couple of surprising small cities along the way.

LODGINGS—Standard motels around Nashville, Bloomington and Columbus. Other choices: In Nashville, the Artists Colony Inn, airy rooms with locally crafted furnishings, downtown (doubles from $107). In Brown County State Park, Abe Martin Lodge, motel-style rooms or cozy cabins (also hearty, home-style meals; doubles from $69). In Bloomington, The Grant Street Inn (doubles from $100) and Scholars Inn (doubles from $110), both bed and breakfasts. In Spring Mill State Park, Spring Mill Inn, comfortable lodge rooms in a historic building (also good dining; doubles from $69). In Columbus, the Columbus Inn bed and breakfast, classically furnished rooms in the beautifully renovated 1895 City Hall (doubles from $96). In Morgantown, The Rock House, an eccentric, Victorian-style home (doubles from $75).

CAMPING—In Brown County State Park. Also, near Bloomington, along Lake Monroe, more than 300 campsites.

DINING—In Nashville, the Nashville House, fried chicken, fried biscuits and other homey favorites; Hob Nob Corner for hearty breakfasts. In Bloomington, Chapman's for elegant,

most visited park. You can drive to Hesitation Point, one of several over-looks. Along the way, picnic tables perch on grassy hillsides—perfect spots to glimpse white-tailed deer grazing in the surrounding woods. Ten miles of hiking trails scale hills and descend into forests.

Drive 8 miles west on State-46.

③ T.C. Steele State Historic Site

Some historians credit early 1900s landscape painter T.C. Steele with founding Brown County's art colony. Steele's home and studio, surrounded by lush gardens, sit on a hilltop. You can tour the cottage, known as the House of the Singing Winds. It's filled with Steele's paintings and furnished just as it was when he died in 1927.

More paintings hang in the barnlike studio. Old-fashioned flowers fill the gardens. You can follow trails through woods and wildflower patches.

Continue 7 miles west on State-46.

④ Bloomington

(Population: 60,630) In this pretty uni-versity city, visitors sample the shop-ping and attend Indiana Univer-sity (IU) events. Revitalized down-town Bloomington unfolds along the wide, shady streets. Shops and restau-rants line the courthouse square at Bloomington's center. One popular visitor stop is the Bloomington Antique Mall, the largest in southern Indiana. You can browse and buy at 120 booths there.

On the sprawling, tree-shaded IU campus, the Lilly Library boasts an extensive collection of rare books, including a Gutenberg Bible. The IU Art Museum, a work of art itself, includes more than 30,000 master-pieces that span the centuries. Alumni and fans flock to Bloomington for uni-versity events on weekends, so check ahead if you plan to stay overnight.

Backtrack 3 miles east on State-46 and drive 7 miles south on State-446.

⑤ Lake Monroe

Quiet reigns in the shallower waters of this 19-mile-long manmade reservoir,

Indiana's largest. East of the State-446 causeway, regulations restrict boats to idling speed. By June, lily pads carpet tranquil inlets, and you may spot eagles tending their young.

Power boaters zip across the lake's deeper waters west of State-446. Stop at the visitors center north of the bridge for information about parks and camp-sites along Lake Monroe's shore. With waterfront campsites, a beach and a marina, the nearby Paynetown State Recreation Area serves as a gateway to the lake's west side.

Drive 10 miles south on State-446. Turn southwest on State-58 and continue for 10 miles.

⑥ Bedford

(Population: 13,810) This hardwork-ing town calls itself the "Limestone Capital of the World." Around the town, the huge holes you see mark sites where miners removed chunks of the gray rock. Bedford limestone built New York City's Empire State Build-ing and many of the federal offices in Washington, D.C. Elliott Special Pro-ducts, a quarry operation west of town, gives tours on Saturdays.

Just south of Bedford along US-50, the world's largest underground river flows in Blue Springs Caverns Park. Electric tour boats take visitors more than a mile into the caverns' interior, where lights reveal rare blind cave fish and eerie rock formations.

Drive 10 miles south from Bedford on State-37. Turn east on State-60 and drive about 1 mile.

⑦ Mitchell

(Population: 4,770) Antiques shops cluster along the main street of this quiet farming community. The 1906 Opera House hosts performances all year, ranging from jazz concerts to children's plays.

Continue 3 miles east on State-60.

⑧ Spring Mill State Park

Just east of Mitchell at Spring Mill State Park, log homes, an apothecary shop and an old-time post office form a restored pioneer village that surrounds a working 1816 corn and saw mill.

Brown County
State Park,
16,000 acres
in the center
of the county.

Drop in at the park's massive sandstone Spring Mill Inn. It's been a popular dining and overnight stop for more than 50 years.

Drive 22 miles southeast on State-60.

Salem

(Population: 5,620) Travelers from all over trace their family trees in the nationally recognized genealogy library at Salem's John Hay Center/Stevens Memorial Museum. The center also includes a re-created pioneer village that you can tour. On Sundays in spring and summer, sprint cars zip around the town's speedway.

Drive 23 miles north on State-135. Jog 3 miles west on US-50 and continue 20 miles north on State-135. This route, one of the state's most scenic, takes you back to Brown County through the wooded hills of Hoosier National Forest.

Story

(Population: 7) As you might guess from the population count, progress overlooked this tiny Brown County hamlet. The old general store, a rustic-looking yesteryear structure still sided in tin, now welcomes travelers as The Story Inn, with a good restaurant and simple accommodations. Old-time gas pumps greet you out front. Inside, wooden shelves line the walls, filled with sturdy 19th-century crocks and antique tools.

Drive 4½ miles northeast on State-135. At Stone Head, drive northeast on Bellsville Pike Road. (Perhaps a town once existed at Stone Head, but all that remains today is a century-old stone highway marker carved in the shape of a man's head.) Continue 11 more miles northeast on Bellsville Pike Road. Then, drive 5 miles east on State-46.

Columbus

(Population: 31,800) Though it's located just a half-hour east of Nashville, Columbus seems worlds away. More than 50 masterpieces of 20th-century architecture—all angles and glass—soar over the city's flower-lined streets. Columbus ranks sixth in the nation in the number of significant buildings designed by noted architects.

It all started almost four decades ago, when Columbus' leading employer, Cummins Engine Company, paid a top architect to design a local school. Since then, the company has sponsored other prominent and talented architects—from I.M. Pei to Richard Meier—who've designed Columbus' public buildings, churches and schools.

Board a bus at the downtown visitors center for a tour of the city's architectural landmarks, including a glass-walled mall and a church with a spire so tall, it almost needed an aircraft-warning blinker.

Golfers consistently rank the city's 18-hole Otter Creek Golf Course, 6 miles east of town off State-46, one of the nation's top 25 public courses.

North of town along I-65, you can shop at the Manufacturers Marketplace outlet mall, which includes more than 70 discount stores.

Drive 11 miles north on I-65. Take Exit 80 and drive 2 miles west on State-252. Drive 4 miles north on US-31 and 13 miles west on State-252.

Morgantown

(Population: 980) Victorian homes preside over Washington Street at the center of this sleepy farm town. From the curb, The Rock House looks much like its neighbors. But get closer, and you'll see the 1894 home's rock walls serve as a scrapbook for the family who built it.

Shards of pottery, bits of jewelry, doorknobs and even old photographs are embedded in the concrete between the stones. Current owners Donna and George Williams have transformed the 13-room home into a bed and breakfast. Down the street, the House of Clocks sells antique timepieces.

Drive 7½ miles south on State-135 to Beanblossom. (The only sign of a town here is an open-air, roadside produce stand.) Jog southwest on Covered Bridge Road to cross the century-old Beanblossom covered bridge—it's rickety-looking, but still deemed sound. If you feel adventurous, drive across. After less than a mile, the gravel track rejoins State-135. The town of Nashville is just 4 miles south. ■

By Barbara Briggs Morrow.

HOMEMADE
CANDIES AND FUDGE

THE
HARVEST
PRESERVE

PRESERVED HERE
JELLIES · JAMS · BUTTERS

HOMEMADE
ICE CREAM

CIRRUS
AUTOMATED TELLER SERVICE
Bank

ONE
WAY

Signs point the
way for visitors
in Nashville.

HIDDEN HILLS AND VALLEYS

The lush, rolling hills and river valleys of south-central Wisconsin have been attracting newcomers for generations. Cornish miners came in the 1840s, hoping to strike it rich. The fertile landscape reminded Swiss dairy farmers who settled here of home. Years later, the area's natural beauty captivated visionary architect Frank Lloyd Wright, who built his studio, Taliesin, near the town of Spring Green.

Ethnic heritage and pride thrive in communities throughout the region. In New Glarus, a community where chalets with intricate gingerbread trim greet you, some locals still speak the Swiss/German dialect of their ancestors and create delicate Old World patterns in lace. Around the nearby town of Monroe, dairy cows graze contentedly on the hillsides, and cheese-making remains a time-honored art. You can watch mild baby Swiss and pungent Limburger being made.

Years ago, rich ore deposits in this region created prosperous mining communities such as Mineral Point, where visitors today can tour 150-year-old mining-boom homes and sample hearty Cornish pasties. In Platteville, to the southwest, you can catch a ride on an authentic mine train, even venture underground to explore a bona fide lead mine.

Begin and end your easy-driving, 200-mile circle tour through this historic region of wooded hills and deep, green valleys in Madison. Wisconsin's vibrant capital city is situated amid four sparkling lakes. But be forewarned: You're likely to get sidetracked along the way by scenic backroads, lazy rivers just right for canoeing and tubing, lakes brimming with fish, inviting hiking and bicycling trails, and panoramic views that stretch to distant counties.

The old lead-mining town of Mineral Point today claims an artists' colony.

❶ Madison

(Population: 194,600) The capitol dome that towers above the Madison skyline guides visitors to the heart of Wisconsin's energetic capital city. Downtown Madison occupies an isthmus that separates Lake Mendota and Lake Monona. The University of Wisconsin (UW) campus and its 41,000 student population lend the culturally rich city an irrepressible spirit.

In summer, Madison's Capitol Square provides the perfect setting for Saturday morning farmers markets. Weather permitting, step out on the capitol dome's observation platform for a sweeping view of the city skyline.

From the square, you can stroll down the State Street pedestrian mall, filled with trendy—some might say unusual—shops, galleries and coffeehouses. Ahead, the UW campus ascends Bascom Hill and continues for miles along the shores of Lake Mendota. At the student union, sample famous Babcock ice cream, which the UW Dairy Science Department makes. Then, stroll the wooded lakeshore path that leads through campus.

From campus, follow Monroe Street southwest to Nakoma Road, till Nakoma meets Verona Road (US-18/151). Drive 6 miles west to State-69; follow State-69 south 18 miles.

❷ New Glarus

(Population: 1,760) Chalet-type architecture signals your arrival in New Glarus, known as "Little Switzerland," a town Swiss immigrants settled in 1845. Shops sell local crafters' works and Swiss imports. Stop by the New Glarus Bakery and Tea Room and Schoco-Laden sweet shop. Weekdays, you can tour the New Glarus Brewing Company. Three markets in town sell Swiss- and German-style meats.

Drive 16 miles south on State-69.

❸ Monroe

(Population: 10,240) You can't go far before discovering a cheese factory or

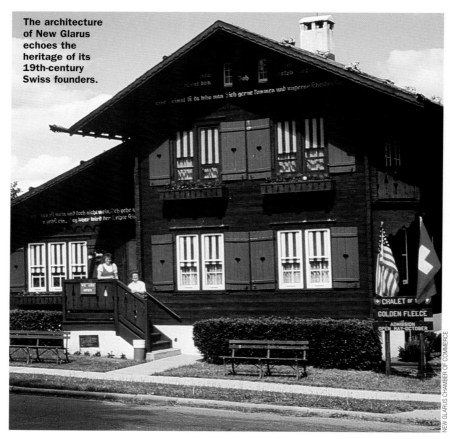

The architecture of New Glarus echoes the heritage of its 19th-century Swiss founders.

NEW GLARUS CHAMBER OF COMMERCE

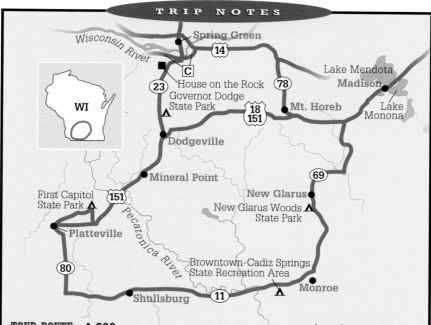

TOUR ROUTE—A 200-mile loop through the hills of south-central Wisconsin, visiting towns rich in ethnic heritage and mining lore.

LODGINGS—Standard motels are plentiful in Madison. Other choices: In Madison, The Collins House (doubles from $120) and Mansion Hill Inn bed and breakfasts (doubles from $100). In New Glarus, the castle-like New Glarus Hotel (doubles from $44) and low-slung Chalet Land-haus (doubles from $68), both also feature Swiss dining. Near Platteville, The Wisconsin House Stage Coach Inn, once a stagecoach stop (doubles from $55). Near Spring Green, The Springs Golf Club Resort (doubles from $179).

CAMPING—New Glarus Woods State Park, south of New Glarus. Governor Dodge State Park, north of Dodgeville.

DINING—In Madison, the Blue Marlin for fresh fish; Wild Iris Cafe for pasta specials; Quivey's Grove (south of Madison) for specialties made from local ingredients; Smoky's or Mariner's Inn for steak; Casa de Lara for Mexican fare. In New Glarus, the New Glarus Hotel and Glarner Stube for Swiss specialties. In Mineral Point, The Red Rooster Cafe, for Cornish pasties (meat pies).

CELEBRATIONS—In Madison, Paddle and Portage race, third weekend in July (608/255-1008). In New Glarus, the Wilhelm Tell Festival, re-enacting the story of Swiss independence, Labor Day weekend (800/527-6838). In Monroe, Cheese Days, third weekend in September in even-numbered years (608/325-7648).

INFORMATION—*Wisconsin Dept. of Tourism, Box 7976, Madison, WI 53707 (800/432-8747); Greater Madison Convention & Visitors Bureau, 615 E. Washington Ave., Madison, WI 53703 (800/373-6376); New Glarus Tourism & Advertising, Box 713, New Glarus, WI 53574 (800/527-6838); Monroe Area Chamber of Commerce, 1505 Ninth St., Monroe, WI 53566 (608/325-7648); Platteville Chamber of Commerce, 275 Hwy. 151W, Platteville, WI 53818 (608/348-8888); Mineral Point Chamber of Commerce, 225 High St., Box 78, Mineral Point, WI 53565 (608/987-3201); Spring Green Area Chamber of Commerce, Box 3, Spring Green, WI 53588 (800/588-2042).*

cheese shop in Monroe, the self-pro-claimed "Swiss Cheese Capital of the World." Visitors can watch cheese made—holes and all—at the Franklin Cheese Factory along Franklin Road or Roth Kase along State-69S. While in town, send a cheese "care package" home from one of the many shops. Stately Victorian-era buildings line the old town square. The giant, Romanesque building is the Green County Courthouse.

Drive 8 miles west on State-11.

❹ Browntown-Cadiz Springs State Recreation Area

Road signs lead you 1½ miles into this 629-acre recreation area. The park includes two popular fishing lakes. Bird-watchers can spot great blue herons and other migrating waterfowl along Zanders Lake Nature Trail.

Drive 25 miles west on State-11.

❺ Shullsburg

(Population: 1,240) The lead-mining rush of 1827 brought fortune seekers to the mineral-rich Shullsburg area. Nearby towns bear telltale names such as Lead Mine and New Diggings. For warmth and shelter, the miners carved crude dugouts called "badger holes" into the hillsides, giving the Badger State its nickname. Learn more about the region's mining history at the small Badger Mine and Museum (fol-low the signs along State-11).

Drive 10 miles west on State-11 to State-80, then go 12 miles north.

❻ Platteville

(Population: 9,580) At Platteville's Mining Museum, visitors descend 55 feet into a lead mine and tour its maze of limestone tunnels. Historians say lead-mining tunnels may lie below half of the historic town, rimmed by hills. Back aboveground, you can ride inside authentic ore cars aboard a mine train that a locomotive pulls.

Nearby, at UW-Platteville, Chicago Bears fans watch their favorite team practice mid-July to mid-August.

From the Mining Museum, drive 6 miles northeast on County-B.

❼ First Capitol State Park and Belmont Mound State Park

In 1835, this high ridge site served as capital of the Wisconsin Territory, which encompassed all of present-day Wisconsin, Iowa and Minnesota, and part of North Dakota and South Dakota. Free summertime guided tours take you inside the original white-clapboard Council House and Supreme Court buildings.

You can stop for a picnic with scenic views at Belmont Mound State Park, just across the road.

Drive 3 miles southeast on County-G to US-151. Drive 12 miles northeast.

❽ Mineral Point

(Population: 2,430) More than 900 buildings in this old mining town, now a mecca for artists and crafters, appear in the National Register of Historic Places. Brick and honey-colored lime-stone buildings line downtown's High Street. The street extends beneath the gaze of the town's mascot: a pointer dog cast in zinc at the former Wisconsin Power and Light building.

The State Historical Society offers tours of Pendarvis, an area of restored homes where Cornish miners lived.

Around town, studios, galleries, antiques shops, and bed and breakfasts welcome visitors. Follow Commerce Street to the east edge of town, and you'll come to the trailhead of the Cheese Country Trail. The hiking and biking route roughly parallels the Pecatonica River for 47 miles south-east to Monroe.

Drive 5 miles east of Mineral Point on US-151. Exit at State-23N and drive 6 miles north through Dodgeville.

❾ Governor Dodge State Park

The wooded terrain of this park, 4 miles north of Dodgeville, consists of valleys and steep hills. The park in-cludes lakes, two campgrounds, 35 miles of hiking trails, even 22 miles of horseback trails.

Drive 10 miles north on State-23. You'll pass House on the Rock, an

The capitol in Madison, a Wisconsin landmark.

ZANE WILLIAMS/THIRD COAST

intriguing stop. It sits atop a steep, rocky outcropping. Eclectic collections that fill the rooms and halls include everything from pipe organs to toy soldiers and a magnificent carousel.

⑩ Spring Green

(Population: 1,270) This area is best known for the famous architect Frank Lloyd Wright, who lived here. Taliesin (pronounced talley-ESSen), the compound where Wright lived and worked, opens its doors to visitors. You can tour Wright's home, nearby Hillside School and the Taliesin grounds. Stop at the visitors center near where State-23 meets County-C.

A little farther east along County-C, the American Players Theatre performs Shakespeare's works beneath summer skies. Backtrack on County-C and continue north on State-23 to downtown Spring Green. Wright's students and associates designed many of the town's galleries and buildings.

Drive 20 miles east on US-14, then 7 miles south on State-78.

⑪ Mount Horeb

(Population 3,250) Stop at this friendly farming town to see the Wisconsin Folk Museum, filled with arts and crafts. The Mount Horeb Mustard Museum contains 1,300 varieties. Next door, Witchery Stitchery sells fine needle crafts; Open House Imports stocks Norwegian gift items.You can buy custom-made teddy bears at Hollowlog Collectibles.

Mount Horeb anchors a region ripe with things to do. All lie off US-18/151W (pick it up just south of town). Explore Cave of the Mounds, a cavern where you can take daily guided tours. West from there, costumed guides at Little Norway lead tours of an 1856 Norwegian farmstead.

Blue Mound State Park, farther west, includes hiking trails and hilltop towers, from which you can see for miles.

Drive 20 miles east of Mount Horeb on US-18/151, returning to Madison to complete your tour. ■

By Tina Lassen.

LAKE SUPERIOR'S NORTH SHORE

Fishermen and loggers came to Minnesota's north shore more than a century ago. Even today, the woodsy corridor that runs along Lake Superior from Duluth north into Canada remains at the edge of a vast wilderness. US-61 provides almost the only link to serene harbor towns and state parks along the shore and to the wild country beyond.

All along the way on this 175-mile lakeshore tour, time-worn cliffs rise like weathered castles, their walls battered by crashing waves from the world's largest freshwater lake. Inland, vast woodlands of aspen, maple and pine, most protected within Superior National Forest, blanket 10,000 square miles of Minnesota's northeast tip.

Tree-covered hills of the Sawtooth Mountain Range, which formed the shore of Lake Superior before the water receded eons ago, now rise several miles inland. More than two dozen rivers rush from these highlands to the lake, transforming the shore into a magical realm of waterfalls. Within steps of the highway (a smooth two-lane for most of the trip), crystal rivulets trickle from canyons, and mist-shrouded torrents roar through deep crevices.

An artists' colony thrives in Grand Marais, toward the north end of the route. The once remote fishing village now brims with shops and galleries. Talk to shopkeepers and artists, and you'll hear different versions of the same story: The more they visited Minnesota's north shore, the harder it became to leave.

Split Rock Lighthouse, open to visitors, once guided ships on Lake Superior.

----------❶----------
Duluth

(Population: 85,500) A decade of downtown and waterfront revitalization has energized this already colorful port city. Duluth serves as the north shore's traditional gateway. From Lake Superior's western tip, at the mouth of the St. Louis River, the town follows the lakeshore for 17 miles and extends just a few miles inland. Ocean-going freighters, some 1,000 feet or longer, dock in the shadows of giant grain-storage facilities.

Duluth's outskirts loom hundreds of feet overhead in the surrounding hills. Skyline Drive follows the ridge that rims the entire city to Enger Tower, a five-story lookout. Streets plunge steeply from these ridges through downtown, past the 1890s depot, home of four museums and the North Shore Scenic Railroad. Some sightseers prefer to board the train for trips along Lake Superior's shoreline. The train takes you north to Two Harbors *(see No. 2)*, with more than a

2-hour layover for exploring before you return to Duluth.

Duluth's Lakewalk, a 3-mile-long path, parallels the waterfront. You can stroll from the cavernous Fitger's Brewery, restored as an inn and shopping complex, to the Aerial Lift Bridge. The span links the shore and Park Point, the narrow sliver of sand that protects the harbor. Bells clang as the bridge rises 138 feet in just a few seconds, and crowds gather to watch giant ships glide by.

Stroll a little farther along the Lakewalk to the *William A. Irvin*, a freighter you can tour. Nearby, visitors board excursion boats that cruise to the harbor's opposite shore.

The quickest route north is a new, four-lane stretch of US-61 that travels 21 miles north to the town of Two Harbors. But for the best views, follow old US-61, the North Shore Scenic Drive.

----------❷----------
Two Harbors

(Population: 3,650) With the North Shore's first lighthouse and a wide,

Owners Tim and Nancy Ramey in the striking Naniboujou Lodge dining room.

LAYNE KENNEDY

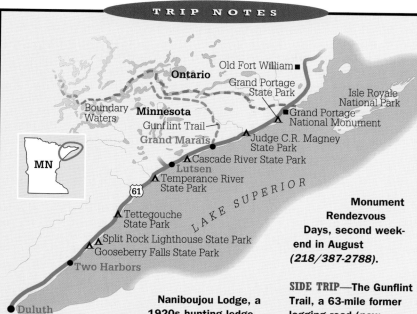

Old Fort William ■
Ontario
Grand Portage
State Park
Isle Royale
National Park
Boundary **Minnesota**
Waters
Gunflint Trail— ■ Grand Portage
National Monument
Grand Marais
Judge C.R. Magney
State Park
MN
Cascade River State Park
Lutsen
Temperance River
State Park
61
LAKE SUPERIOR
Tettegouche
State Park
Split Rock Lighthouse State Park
Gooseberry Falls State Park
Two Harbors
Duluth

TOUR ROUTE—A 175-mile lakeside route between harbor towns and state parks from Duluth north to Canada.

LODGINGS—Standard motels in Duluth and Grand Marais. Other choices: In Duluth, Fitger's Inn, 60 classically furnished rooms and suites in a renovated brewery on the Lake Superior shore (doubles from $105); The Mansion, 10 guest rooms in a shoreside manor that a mining baron once owned (doubles from $95). Near Lutsen, Blue Fin Bay along Lake Superior, new two-story townhomes with kitchens and fireplaces, steps from the water (townhomes from $120). In Lutsen, Lutsen Resort, one of Minnesota's oldest, with a classic log lodge and more than a mile of Lake Superior frontage (doubles from $75). In Grand Marais,

Naniboujou Lodge, a 1920s hunting lodge transformed into a pampering hotel, known for colorful Cree designs in the dining room (doubles from $69).

CAMPING—At Gooseberry Falls and Cascade River state parks.

DINING—In Duluth, Grandma's for thick, juicy burgers; the Pickwick, a Duluth institution on the waterfront, for walleye and grilled steaks. In Two Harbors, Shari's Kitchen, a combination cafe and antiques shop, a perfect lunch stop. In Grand Marais, Birch Terrace Supper Club for fresh lake fish in an 1800s lumber baron's home; The Blue Water Cafe, a casual eatery near the waterfront.

CELEBRATIONS—In Duluth, Grandma's Marathon, including waterfront entertainment, third weekend in June (800/4-DULUTH). Grand Portage National

Monument Rendezvous Days, second weekend in August (218/387-2788).

SIDE TRIP—The Gunflint Trail, a 63-mile former logging road (now paved), takes you from Grand Marais northwest to the Boundary Waters Canoe Area. This paradise for outdoor lovers along the Canadian border includes more than 1,000 lakes. Many of the 16 lodges along the trail supply equipment and guides. *Gunflint Trail Assoc., Box 205, Grand Marais, MN 55604 (800/338-6932).*

INFORMATION—*Minnesota Office of Tourism, 100 Metro Square Bldg., 121 Seventh Pl. E., St. Paul, MN 55101 (800/657-3700); Duluth Convention & Visitors Bureau, 100 Lake Place Dr., Duluth, MN 55802 (800/4-DULUTH); Lutsen-Tofte Tourism Assoc., Box 2248, Tofte, MN 55615 (888/61-NORTH); Grand Marais Chamber of Commerce, Box 1048, Grand Marais, MN 55604 (800/622-4014).*

deep bay, this shore town prospered as a major port for freighters loading ore hauled by rail from Minnesota's Iron Range. At the harbor, you'll see the world's largest ore dock. The Edna G. is berthed nearby. At the time of the Edna G.'s retirement, it was the last steam tug still operating on Lake Superior.

The town's turn-of-the-century depot, overlooking the harbor, now serves as a museum. The 1892 lighthouse is a museum, too.

You can stop at the visitors center on the north end of town to pick up a walking-tour map of more than a dozen historic buildings. They include the original office of corporate giant 3M (Minnesota Mining and Manufacturing), which once headquartered here, and the 1937 band shell, where one of the nation's oldest municipal bands performs during the summer months.

Drive 13 miles northeast on US-61.

❸ Gooseberry Falls State Park

Easy trails lead from roadside parking to picnic spots and five glistening waterfalls, including one that plunges 110 feet. Stop at the park-run Nature Store for information about the park and other north shore sites.

Drive 7 miles northeast on US-61.

❹ Split Rock Lighthouse State Park

This 1910 lighthouse sits atop a cliff that rises 170 feet above Lake Superior. No all-weather road extended to this part of the lakeshore until 1923, so the lighthouse builders brought what materials they needed by ship and laboriously hoisted them up the face of a sheer cliff.

Now, you can the climb the tower and examine the giant lens that helped guide ships until 1969. Next door, the lightkeeper's residence, restored to its 1924 appearance, also is open for tours. A history center features exhibits about Lake Superior navigation, shipwrecks and a short film about the lighthouse.

More than 12 miles of trails lead from this area to secluded campsites

and down to the rocky shore.

Continue about 15 miles northeast on US-61.

❺ Tettegouche State Park

Hike a mile from the highway along the Baptism River to one of the highest waterfalls in Minnesota. Another trail leads you to Shovel Point, a cliff jutting into Lake Superior. Be sure to watch for wild blueberries and strawberries that grow along the path.

Drive 24 miles northeast, still following US-61.

❻ Temperance River State Park

Waters of the Temperance River race through a craggy gorge on their way to Lake Superior. Just east of the highway, a catwalk crosses the roiling stream. Eight miles of trails follow the river inland to rocky ledges that overlook the canyon below.

Drive 10 miles northeast on US-61. About 7 miles north of the state park, drive Forest Road-336 north 4 miles to the Oberg Mountain and Leveaux trails, which take you to overlooks 1,000 feet above Lake Superior.

❼ Lutsen

(*Population: 20*) A handful of resorts makes up this community at the foot of Moose Mountain. Lutsen's Resort, one of Minnesota's oldest, has welcomed visitors for four generations.

Skiers flock here in winter months. But when the weather warms, gondolas take you on a scenic trip to the summit, 800 feet above Lake Superior. From this height, you can see for 100 miles on a clear day.

Drive 10 miles northeast on US-61.

❽ Cascade River State Park

This 2,800-acre state park gets its name from a series of waterfalls that stairsteps down toward Lake Superior. From the park's footbridge, you can see five of the falls tumbling down the rocky gorge.

Eighteen miles of trails wind along both sides of the river gorge. You can

In Duluth's
harbor, the Aerial
Lift Bridge rises
138 feet in seconds.

follow the path to Lookout Mountain, 500 feet above Lake Superior, for a view of the whole valley.

Drive 8 miles northeast on US-61.

Grand Marais

(Population: 1,170) Once a fishing village, Grand Marais has become the home of a thriving artists' colony. The town frames a natural harbor that bustles with pleasure craft in summer. Gulls circle and dive overhead and waddle alongside delighted visitors. Several charter companies offer fishing excursions.

In this community, you can settle into motels that are just steps from the water, then walk to nearby shops and galleries. The harborside Trading Post, a two-story cedar structure, sells everything from local crafters' works to jackets and camping gear. Artists' renderings of moody Lake Superior fill Sivertson Gallery, a converted cottage that's a couple of blocks away beside the lake.

The Johnson Heritage Post Gallery, a new log structure, displays the works of Anna C. Johnson, one of the area's best known artists.

Sightseers stroll the breakwater that leads to a small lighthouse. Along the way, be on the lookout for names etched into the rock as long ago as 1892. Another trail takes you to a potholed shelf of volcanic rock that edges the lake—a perfect spot for a picnic and watching freighters crawl along the horizon.

For a sweeping view of the town and harbor, make the easy 1-mile climb to Sweetheart's Bluff, which rises at the edge of Grand Marais.

Drive 18 miles northeast on US-61.

Judge C.R. Magney State Park

A 2-mile trail climbs along the steep banks of the Brule River to a roaring 50-foot-high waterfall and a mysterious spot known as Devil's Kettle. Water from the falls flows into this hole in the bedrock and disappears, stumping experts who've tried to discover where the stream leads.

Drive another 20 miles northeast on US-61.

Grand Portage State Park

Minnesota's newest state park, which opened in 1994, is just south of the Canadian border. A half-mile trail follows the Pigeon River to a viewing platform at High Falls, where the water cascades 120 feet.

Drive 7 miles northeast on US-61.

Grand Portage National Monument

Costumed park staffers play the roles of French-Canadian voyageurs and their Ojibwa partners at this re-created 1700s fur-trading post along the lakeshore. You might meet a buckskinshirted voyageur cooking over an open fire or an Ojibwa woman beading a pair of moccasins.

Four buildings within the stockade include the Great Hall, where you can see replicas of the early traders' clothing and weapons.

Outside the stockade, a trail leads to Mount Rose, where an overlook puts you 300 feet above the bay. A passenger ferry travels daily from the compound's dock to Isle Royale National Park, a 45-mile-long island wilderness some 18 miles offshore. Isle Royale is home to wolves, moose and other wild creatures *(see "Splendors of the Keweenaw Peninsula," page 4).*

Drive 26 miles northeast, across the Canadian border on Ontario-61.

Old Fort William

In 1803, when British traders abandoned Grand Portage in what's now Minnesota, they retreated to this fort. Some 42 reconstructed buildings, including an Ojibwa camp and a working farm, bring that adventurous era back to life. Walking tours and wagon rides leave regularly from the visitors center. You also can try your hand at paddling a voyageur's canoe.

Most travelers who follow the north shore route head back to Duluth after visiting Old Fort William. Take your time on the return trip; you'll enjoy viewing the scenery along the lakeshore again and again. ■

By Barbara Briggs Morrow.

In Tettegouche
State Park, one of
Minnesota's
highest falls.

MARK TWAIN'S REALM

It's almost impossible to mention Missouri or the Mississippi River without conjuring up images of Tom Sawyer, Huck Finn, riverboats, whitewashed fences and carefree summer fun.

Samuel Clemens (a.k.a. Mark Twain) drew upon his boyhood experiences in the Mississippi River town of Hannibal to create these timeless images. And, just as his 19th-century hometown shaped young Clemens, America's most famous author solidified Hannibal's place in history. Today, Hannibal's historic downtown retains the air of a quiet, yesteryear hamlet, riding the current of a lazy river. The world's most famous whitewashed fence gently slopes toward the Mississippi along Hill Street. The riverboat *Mark Twain* takes visitors on daily cruises. On this tour, you'll also visit Twain's birthplace—a humble, two-room cabin near what's now a giant lake—and travel to Keokuk, Iowa, where young Clemens lived, worked and launched his literary career.

Other locations along or near this stretch of the river also prospered during Twain's time. Mormon founder Joseph Smith considered the town of Nauvoo, Illinois, to be his followers' "New Jerusalem." Tiny Bethel, Missouri, began as a German utopian community some 150 years ago. Merchants in Quincy, Illinois, created an up-and-coming port city, which today boasts 2,000 buildings on the National Register of Historic Places.

These are just a few of the sites that beckon near Twain's mighty river, as it rolls along between southeast Iowa and northwest Missouri on one side and central Illinois on the other. This meandering 230-mile drive on both sides of the Mississippi is like slipping between the covers of Twain's novels and sharing the adventures of his famous characters.

The riverboat *Mark Twain* cruises from Hannibal.

❶ Keokuk

(Population: 13,500) Mark Twain country begins in Iowa's southernmost city. The author came to Keokuk in 1855 to help his brother, Orion, at his Main Street printing shop. Later, in 1889, Twain bought his mother a home here. The Mark Twain Center at the Keokuk Public Library maintains a collection of Twain memorabilia.

Like Twain, Keokuk grew up with the Mississippi. The compact town nestles along an oxbow in the river. Wealth from the Mississippi River traffic created fine homes and public buildings that remain today.

The Miller House Museum displays this early heritage, and St. John's Episcopal Church vividly reflects the wealth of that time. Light pours through two Tiffany stained-glass windows, revealing a ceiling that resembles the upside-down keel of a ship.

Both landmarks can be found between historic Grand Avenue, a mile-long stretch of Victorian homes along the river bluff, and Keokuk's Main Street, a collection of antiques and craft shops. Pick up a walking-tour map from the Tourism Office at 401 Main Street.

The Mississippi still influences Keokuk's daily life. At Lock and Dam 19, adjacent to the city's downtown, you can watch towboats passing through the 1,200-foot-long lock, the biggest step (38 feet) of the 27 locks on the river. The George M. Verity Riverboat Museum, in the riverfront Victory Park, gives you a glimpse of Twain's experiences when he left Keokuk to become a river pilot.

Cross the Mississippi on US-136 to Hamilton, Illinois. Then, drive 11 miles north on State-96.

❷ Nauvoo

(Population: 1,130) Though not a part of Twain country, historic Nauvoo is a worthwhile detour north across the river to Illinois. The riverside hamlet became Illinois' largest city in the 1840s, after Mormon leader Joseph

You can feast at Bethel's Fest Hall Restaurant.

FRANK OBERLE

(314/221-2477);
Autumn Historic Folklife Festival, the third weekend in October
(573/221-2477).

SIDE TRIP—In Illinois, visit Pere Marquette State Park and Lodge, along State-100. Cross the Mississippi River on the US-54 bridge at Louisiana, Missouri, and go 60 miles southeast via State-96 and State-100. The 7,900-acre park, overlooking the Illinois River, offers lodge rooms, cabins and campsites (doubles from $63; 618/786-2331). Elsah, 9 miles farther south along State-100, resembles a New England village beside Mississippi River bluffs (618/465-6676).

INFORMATION—*Missouri Div. of Tourism, Box 1055, Jefferson City, MO 65102 (800/877-1234); Nauvoo Tourism, Box 41, Nauvoo, IL 62354 (217/453-6648); Hannibal Convention & Visitors Bureau, Box 624, 505 N. Third St., Hannibal, MO 63401 (573/221-2477); Western Illinois Tourism Development, 2900 E. Jackson St., Macomb, IL 61455 (309/837-7460); Quincy Convention & Tourism Bureau, 300 Civic Center Plaza, Quincy, IL 62301 (800/97-VISIT); Keokuk Area Convention & Tourism Bureau, 401 Main St., Keokuk, IA 52632 (800/383-1219).*

TOUR ROUTE—A 230-mile, mostly riverside route from Keokuk, Iowa, to Clarksville, Missouri.

LODGINGS—Standard motels in Keokuk, Quincy and Hannibal. Other choices: In Quincy, the Kaufmann House (doubles from $45) and Bueltmann Gasthaus (doubles from $40), both in the historic district. In Hannibal, Garth Woodside Mansion, a pampering bed and breakfast (doubles from $77).

CAMPING—Mark Twain State Park along Mark Twain Lake, near Stoutsville.

DINING—In Keokuk, the Hawkeye Restaurant, great steaks. In Quincy,

Elder's Family Restaurant, a local favorite for good food at modest prices. In Nauvoo, The Old Nauvoo Hotel, noted for its Sunday buffet. In Bethel, Fest Hall Restaurant, home-style cooking. In Hannibal, Huck's Homestead, chicken, catfish and rib buffets nightly.

CELEBRATIONS—In Nauvoo, *The City of Joseph* Outdoor Musical, celebrating Mormon heritage, two weekends in late July, early August (800/453-0022). In Quincy, Germanfest, the last weekend in June (217/224-0037). In Bethel, Quilt Show, in April (816/284-6493). In Hannibal, Mississippi River Art Fair, Memorial Day weekend; National Tom Sawyer Days, the Fourth of July weekend

Smith chose it for his "New Jerusalem." In 6 years, settlers built an all-brick city with 20,000 residents and a $1 million temple. But by 1846, the Mormons abandoned Nauvoo for Utah.

At more than 30 historic sites in the restored settlement of old Nauvoo (a few blocks from downtown), you can see how early Mormons lived, worked and worshiped. The buildings include Joseph Smith's mansion.

Three visitors centers provide walking-tour maps of shops that recreate 1840s products and sell local specialties including Nauvoo blue cheese: Nauvoo Glass Works, Nauvoo Mill and Bakery, woodworking at the Allyn House and Baxter's Winery.

Drive 11 miles south on State-96 to US-136, returning to Keokuk. Along the way, you can stop at Nauvoo State Park, a nice spot for a picnic. Turn left on US-61 in Keokuk. Drive west, then south on US-61 about 20 miles into Missouri. At County-Z, turn right and drive 3 miles southwest to State-81.

--------- **3** ---------

St. Patrick

(Population: 20) The tiny burg of St. Patrick remains the only town in the U.S. that's named for the patron saint of Ireland. A beautiful shrine commemorates him.

Drive 8 miles south on State-81 to rejoin US-61 near Canton. Drive 19 miles south on US-61 to US-24. Go 8 miles east on US-24. You'll pass the riverside Wakonda State Park, with a lake and the largest natural sand beach in Missouri.

--------- **4** ---------

Quincy

(Population: 39,680) High above the river on limestone bluffs, Quincy, Illinois, remained virtually untouched by the 1993 floods. Crossing the new Bayview Bridge from Missouri on US-24, this parklike city of 2,000 historic homes and buildings, many built of stone, spreads out before you.

Ahead along Maine Street is Washington Park, a square block of trees, flowers and a fountain amid a historic district. Nearly 15,000 people gathered here in 1858 to hear a young Abraham Lincoln debate the hometown favorite, Stephen A. Douglas. Each Tuesday

and Saturday during the growing season, the park hosts a farmers market. Exhibits in the Gardner Museum of Architecture and Design, located at the park's southwest corner, explain the town's array of architectural styles.

The central business district, along Maine Street, borders Washington Park on the south. The Yesteryear Antique Mall, at 615 Maine, sells quilts, collectibles, furniture and glassware of more than 50 dealers. Nearby, Scents-n-Things custom-blends bath products.

Stately mansions greet you as you drive east on Maine. *National Geographic* magazine called 16th and Maine the "most architecturally significant corner in the United States," because of its imposing Romanesque, Italianate and Georgian homes. One houses the Quincy Museum of Natural History and Art; another home's carriage house is the location of the Quincy Art Museum.

Backtrack 8 miles to US-61 via the Bayview Bridge (US-24). Drive 9 miles south on US-61/24.

--------- **5** ---------

Palmyra

(Population: 3,371) In the 1860s, Palmyra billed itself as the "handsomest city in north Missouri," thanks to its wealth of antebellum architecture, which still graces this small city. Outside the tan-brick courthouse, a monument remembers 10 Confederate soldiers executed here in 1862. William Russell, the founder of the Pony Express, lies buried in the cemetery just north of town.

Drive 30 miles west on State-168 through Philadelphia and Emden to Shelbyville. Drive 6 miles north on State-15.

--------- **6** ---------

Bethel

(Population: 120) This little town in the Missouri hills began as a German utopian colony in 1844. Colonists abandoned it for Oregon only a year later, but other residents stayed on. Today, the village's historic homes, two-block-long downtown, antiques stores and craft shops harken back to its early heritage. You can watch clay being shaped at the Bethel Colony Pottery and shop for crafts at the Gift

Gaze down on the Mississippi from Lookout Point in Clarksville.

Shop, which doubles as a museum.

Drive 30 miles south on State-15, through Shelbyville to Paris. Drive northeast on US-24 to County-U. Turn right on County-U and go 5 miles east.

Mark Twain Lake and State Park

The 18,600-acre man-made lake and 2,770-acre state park offer camping, hiking and water sports. State-107, State-154 and US-24 provide access to other parts of this giant lake.

Mark Twain Birthplace

In 1835, Mark Twain was born Samuel Clemens in a cabin preserved in the tiny town of Florida *(population: 50)*, at the edge of the state park. The blue, shake-shingled home, part of a state historic site and museum, overlooks Mark Twain Lake. The site houses Twain artifacts and manuscripts.

Drive 6 miles northwest on State-107 to the intersection of US-24. Drive 30 miles northeast on US-24, which becomes US-24/36.

Hannibal

(Population: 18,000) You've arrived in the heart of Twain country, where the author lived from 1839 to 1853. Many Twain sites lie along Hannibal's Main Street. His childhood home, completely restored in 1990, stands at 208 Hill Street, just off Main. Visit the Mark Twain Museum next door, where 16 Norman Rockwell paintings that illustrated editions of *Tom Sawyer* and *Huckleberry Finn* now hang, and the new museum two blocks south.

The author and his characters seem to be everywhere. Lunch at Mark Twain Dinette or thumb through volumes at Becky Thatcher's Bookstore. Within easy walking distance are the Becky Thatcher House, Grant's Drug Store and the law office of Twain's father, Judge Clemens.

Plenty more Twain sites await beyond Hannibal's historic downtown. A statue of Twain overlooks the river atop 300-foot bluffs at Riverview Park, a fine picnic spot north of downtown. Cardiff Hill, which Twain named, lies between the park and downtown. The

famous Tom and Huck Statue stands at the foot of the hill. The Mark Twain Memorial Lighthouse, built in 1935 to honor the 100th anniversary of Twain's birth, towers above.

One-half mile south of the historic district, Lover's Leap provides a sweeping view of the Mississippi. Nearby, you can explore Cameron and Mark Twain caves.

The riverboat *Mark Twain* cruises the river daily (May–October). *Reflections of Mark Twain,* a drama about the author and his famous characters, plays in summer at the Mark Twain Outdoor Theater, just off US-61 south of this small city.

Drive 26 miles southeast on State-79. Limestone bluffs border the Mississippi south of Hannibal. Many soar more than 200 feet.

Louisiana

(Population: 3,967) Founded in 1818 and named to commemorate the Louisiana Purchase, this town begins at the river's edge and climbs up the bluffs on streets named after states.

Settled by southern tobacco growers, Louisiana boasts many pre-Civil War homes. Stark Bro's Nurseries, founded in 1818 and said to be one of the oldest and largest nurseries in the world, anchors the west edge of town along US-54. You can visit founder James Stark's 1816 cabin and shop at Stark's outlet for fruit trees. Louisiana's Victorian commercial district, listed on the National Register of Historic Places, includes antiques shops.

North of Louisiana, along State-79 near Ashburn, Ted Shanks Wildlife Area boasts hiking trails, tours and a visitors center that features exhibits about Mississippi River marsh plants and wildlife.

From Louisiana, drive 8 miles south on State-79.

Clarksville

(Population: 480) Clarksville is another historic river town packed with restored old homes. Artisans sell their creations in shops along Main Street. In winter, more than 300 eagles winter along this stretch of river.■

By Alan Guebert.

Main Street in
Mark Twain's
Hannibal.

TREASURED TOWNS AND HISTORIC VILLAGES

The rolling countryside of east-central Iowa greets you with the same gentle embrace that welcomed the sturdy pioneers who settled here more than a century ago. They came with a dream of religious freedom and a better life. Today, picturesque towns and neighborhoods, as well as Iowa's popular Amana Colonies, dot the peaceful, green landscape. Country roads wind beside fields and meandering rivers.

Handmade creations for sale throughout much of the region evidence the intricate crafting skills that Old World artisans have passed down through the generations. Food traditions run deep here, too. You can feast on sauerbraten and Wiener schnitzel at cozy Amana eateries, *kolaches* at a Czech festival or a juicy Iowa steak at an upscale restaurant.

Your 120-mile route begins in West Branch, boyhood home of former President Herbert Hoover (just off I-80, about 45 miles west of Davenport). From there, you can visit a picture-postcard town that claims America's only college campus listed on the National Register of Historic Places; a thriving Czech neighborhood; and a bustling university community. Amish buggies roll along streets in the farm town of Kalona, not far from the seven Amana Colonies. Founded as a religious communal society in the mid-19th century, the Amanas are Iowa's top visitor attraction today. In between, intriguing turn-offs, backroads and lakeside groves invite you to explore or simply stop and enjoy.

Fruit trees and vines frame the Amana Colonies' Old-World brick architecture.

---------●1---------

West Branch

(Population: 1,870) Just north of I-80, you can follow the steps of Iowa's only president and the nation's 31st commander-in-chief—from the tiny restored cottage of his birth to his final resting place atop a tree-shaded knoll.

Herbert Hoover's gravesite overlooks the Herbert Hoover Presidential Library and Museum, which underwent a $6.5 million renovation 5 years ago. The Colonial-style building chronicles Hoover's life with displays and video presentations.

West Branch's quiet main street and town square are just a block north. Victorian-era brick-and-wood storefronts hold antiques shops, restaurants, and a bed and breakfast.

Drive 8 miles west on I-80 and 17 miles north on State-1.

---------●2---------

Mount Vernon

(Population: 3,500) Tree-lined streets and historic homes welcome you to Mount Vernon, which resembles a New England village as you approach. Take a self-guided tour that includes Iowa's Cornell College, the only U.S. campus listed in its entirety on the National Register of Historic Places. Tour the landmark 1876 King Chapel, with its towering spires and stained glass. Then, browse the shops along the shady main street. The commercial district and the Ash Park neighborhood also appear in the national register.

Drive 13 miles west on US-30 and north on I-380. Along the way, visit the river bluffs at Palisades-Kepler State Park. At Cedar Rapids, follow the signs along I-380 to the Czech Village.

---------●3---------

Cedar Rapids

(Population: 110,000) One-quarter of the residents of this prosperous commercial city along the Cedar River claim Czech or Slovak ancestors. The area reminded them of their European homelands when they settled here.

Today, Cedar Rapids' ethnic community revolves around the Czech

Bicyclists at Herbert Hoover's birthplace in West Branch.

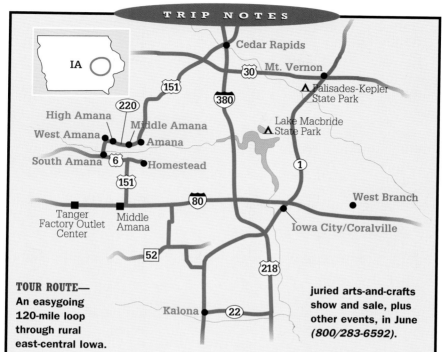

TRIP NOTES

IA

Cedar Rapids

30 Mt. Vernon

151 △ Palisades-Kepler State Park

380

220

High Amana

Middle Amana

West Amana

Amana

Lake Macbride △ State Park

South Amana 6

Homestead

151

1

80

West Branch

Tanger Factory Outlet Center

Middle Amana

Iowa City/Coralville

52

218

TOUR ROUTE— An easygoing 120-mile loop through rural east-central Iowa.

Kalona 22

LODGINGS—Standard motels abound in Cedar Rapids and the Iowa City/Coralville area. Other choices: In Cedar Rapids, the Crowne Plaza Five Seasons Hotel for deluxe lodgings and dining (doubles from $89, weekend packages). In Homestead, Die Heimat Country Inn, rooms with canopy beds and Amana-made furniture (doubles from $46). In Amana, the Guest House Motor Inn, two buildings, one an 1860 sandstone home with modern amenities (doubles from $48). In Iowa City, Haverkamp's Linn Street Homestay, a bed and breakfast, six blocks from downtown (doubles from $40).

CAMPING—Lake Macbride State Park, north of Iowa City. Palisades-Kepler State Park, west of Mount Vernon.

DINING—In Amana, The Ox Yoke Inn Restaurant, smoked pork chops, bratwurst and other hearty German fare. (Many other Amana eateries offer similar-quality dining.) In West Branch, the L&B Steakhouse for fare locals rave about. In Coralville, The Iowa River Power Company, steaks and seafood. In Iowa City, Hamburg Inn No. 2, hearty breakfasts and lunches.

CELEBRATIONS—In Cedar Rapids, Houby (Mushroom) Days in the Czech Village, ethnic dancing and food, weekend after Mother's Day (319/362-8500). In Amana, Woodcrafters Festival, view and buy detailed carvings, mid-June (800/245-5465). In Kalona, fall festival in September (319/656-2669). In Iowa City, Iowa Arts Festival,

juried arts-and-crafts show and sale, plus other events, in June (800/283-6592).

SIDE TRIP—Tanger Factory Outlet Center, discount outlets, 5 miles west of Little Amana along I-80.

INFORMATION—*Eastern Iowa Tourism Assoc., Box 485, Vinton, IA 52349 (800/891-EITA); Mount Vernon Chamber of Commerce, Box 281, Mount Vernon, IA 52314 (319/895-8214); Cedar Rapids Area Convention & Visitors Bureau, Box 5339, Cedar Rapids, IA 52406 (800/735-5557); Amana Colonies Convention & Visitors Bureau, 39 38th Ave., Ste. 100, Amana, IA 52203 (800/245-5465); Kalona Area Chamber of Commerce & Visitors Center, Box 615, Kalona, IA 52247 (319/656-2660); Iowa City/Coralville Convention & Visitors Bureau, 408 First Ave., Coralville, IA 52241 (800/283-6592).*

Village. Take home a taste of the Old World from shops in this two-block area, where you can buy everything from *jaternice* (Bohemian sausage) to imported glassware and *kolaches* (fruit-filled pastries). The National Czech & Slovak Museum & Library displays lavish Old World costumes, glass, jewelry and intricate lace.

Downtown, the Cedar Rapids Museum of Art holds more than 250 of Grant Wood's works. The Iowa painter's stylized renderings of rural life have become American icons.

Cedar Rapids also provides more glimpses of earlier times: the grandeur of Queen Anne architecture and gardens at historic Brucemore mansion and simple pioneer buildings at Ushers Ferry Historic Village, northwest of downtown (both open for tours).

On the way out of town, car buffs—both buyers and browsers—can feast their eyes on the vintage roadsters at Duffy's Collectible Cars showroom (there's a '50s diner next door).

Drive southwest 18 miles on US-151.

Amana Colonies

Fleeing religious oppression, the German, Swiss and Alsatian settlers of the Amana Colonies built a communal society, sharing all work and profits. Founded in 1854, the colonies have since abandoned their communal ways, but the spirit of their society lives in charming villages, filled with antiques, gift shops and German-style restaurants (East Amana has no commercial establishments).

Wandering the quiet streets lined with brick and stone houses, you'll see grapevines clambering over trellises. Wine-making remains an important Amana tradition, and several wineries offer tasting and tours.

Drive ½-mile west on State-220 to the Amana Colonies Visitors Center for the information that you need to explore the seven villages. Backtrack on State-220 to Amana.

Amana

(Population: 550) Craft and specialty shops line the streets in the largest of the Amana Colonies. You can sample

and buy famous Amana ham, bacon and sausage at the Amana Meat Shop & Smokehouse. Then, shop for clothes and fabrics at Iowa's only operating woolen mill. Watch beer being made at the Millstream Brewing Co., Iowa's oldest brewery, where you can taste and buy. The Museum of Amana History houses artifacts the Amanas' original settlers used.

When you finish shopping and exploring, dig into the steaming bowls and platters of delicious German and American food, served family-style at several fine Amana restaurants.

Drive 2 miles west on State-220.

-------- **6** --------
Middle Amana

(Population: 550) Drop by the Hearth Oven Bakery for a scrumptious pastry, and visit the Communal Kitchen and Cooper Shop Museum.

Drive 2 miles west on State-220.

-------- **7** --------
High Amana

(Population: 140) Step back in time at the Old-Fashioned High Amana General Store. The interior still looks much as it did when the store opened 135 years ago.

Drive 1 mile west on State-220.

-------- **8** --------
West Amana

(Population: 125) Watch artisans create brooms and baskets, then buy one at the Broom and Basket Shop.

Drive 1½ miles south on State-220 across the scenic Iowa River.

-------- **9** --------
South Amana

(Population: 150) At the Schanz Furniture and Refinishing Shop, you can buy handmade furnishings of walnut, cherry and oak. Displays range from the White House to an Amana farmstead.

Drive 4½ miles east on US-6.

-------- **10** --------
Homestead

(Population: 140) Former Yankee pitcher Bill Zuber created a mecca for big-league-baseball fans when he opened Bill Zuber's restaurant here. You also can tour Ehrle Brothers

Old Capitol on The University of Iowa campus in Iowa City.

DOUG SMITH

Winery, the oldest in the colonies.

Backtrack 2 miles to US-151 and drive 6 miles south.

---------- 11 ----------

Little Amana

Settle in for the night or buy anything from an Amana sweater to rhubarb wine at this complex of shops, motels and eateries along I-80. Just passing through? Try fast food Amana-style at the Little Amana Bratwurst Haus.

For a scenic countryside junket, drive 5 miles east on I-80, take exit 230 and go 6 miles south on Southwest Blackhawk Road. Drive 3 miles east on Black Diamond Avenue (County-52) and 3 miles south on Orval Yoder Turnpike. Drive 2 miles east on Southwest 500th Street (County-62) and 6 miles south on State-1.

---------- 12 ----------

Kalona

(Population: 1,942) Parked buggies and work shirts flapping on clotheslines testify to the lives without cars and electricity that the Amish lead today.

Kalona's Amish community (not to be confused with the Amana Colonies) flourishes amid rich farmland. Learn more about the Amish at the Kalona Historical Village and on tours that leave from the chamber of commerce. Shops downtown and along the roadways sell quilts and other handicrafts. At Twin County Dairy, watch cheesemaking and buy some to take home.

Drive 9 miles east on State-22 and 8 miles north on US-218 to the Riverside Drive exit. Go 4 miles on Riverside Drive. Turn right on Iowa Avenue.

---------- 13 ----------

Iowa City

(Population: 59,738) The University of Iowa campus sprawls along hills above the Iowa River. You can tour Iowa's onetime capitol, the campus centerpiece. Across the river, the art museum houses works by Picasso and other greats. Downtown Iowa City neighbors the campus, with shops and restaurants lining a pedestrian mall, where you can linger. ■

By Linda Ryberg.

135

HILL COUNTRY MEANDERING

Many Midwesterners forge their only impressions of Illinois from memorable weekends in Chicago or by gazing for hours at what seems to be a vast, green ocean of corn and soybeans nudging up to the Interstate highways across the Prairie State. If you're among that group, you're in for a big surprise when you venture into southern Illinois.

This triangular wedge of woods, water and hills, bounded by the Mississippi and Ohio rivers, is the state's most naturally scenic, rural and least-traveled area. Dark, mysterious cypress and tupelo swamps are alive with wildlife day and night, and may remind you of America's Deep South. Rugged, tree-covered hills and rocky canyons are part of the age-old Ozark Mountains, which spill into southern Illinois. Four flags—Spanish, French, British and, of course, Old Glory—have flown over this region, each culture leaving behind its unique landmarks and traditions.

Southern Illinois hill country is particularly appealing in spring, when the forests turn emerald with delicate, new life. As the weather warms, redbud and dogwood blossoms lend a patrician air to every village you visit. Summertime brings festivals and historic re-enactments. Hiking trails and lakes lace the giant Shawnee National Forest, which claims 270,000 acres in the region and surrounds four state parks and forests.

On this 260-mile route, which begins in historic Maeystown along the Mississippi and ends atop the rugged limestone outcroppings of the Garden of the Gods not far from the Ohio River, a very different Illinois emerges. Like most visitors, you're certain to grow to love this scenic region.

Pomona Natural
Land Bridge
in Shawnee
National Forest.

① Maeystown

(Population: 120) This old German village, tucked amid the Mississippi River bluffs, is so small, it gets overlooked at census time. The entire community, founded in 1852, is a National Historic District. Maeystown's flagstone street gutters, rock-walled terraces and brick buildings reflect German craftsmanship and sturdiness.

In the two-block downtown, the refurbished general store sells antiques, German gifts and crafts. Other businesses, such as the Home Place Farm Bakery, Knobloch Mercantile and the Gift Shop, line Main Street.

Drive 2 miles west from Maeystown along the Maeystown Blacktop to Bluff Road. Turn left on Bluff Road and drive 9 miles southeast to State-155.

② Prairie du Rocher

(Population: 700) Founded in 1722 as the center of Illinois' French colonial district, Prairie du Rocher's wide streets, houses and limestone walls recall that heritage today. Along Main Street, walk past the Creole House, a long, low, French-style home dating to 1800. A few blocks west along State-155, you can visit Village Hall, another classic example of French colonial architecture. Be sure to drop by Annie's, a new flower and crafts shop across the street.

Drive 4 miles west on State-155.

③ Fort de Chartres

Established in 1720, Fort de Chartres became the strongest French fortification in North America when completed in 1753 and served as the seat of French government in the Mississippi River Valley. Visitors can view the limestone walls, chapel and museum. Look for the high water mark on the fort's flag, a legacy of the 1993 flood, which inundated the site.

Backtrack to Prairie du Rocher on State-155 and turn right on Main Street. Drive south along Main Street to Bluff Road. Drive 13 miles south to State-3,

"Colonial-era soldiers" parade at Fort de Chartres.

BARBARA MARTIN

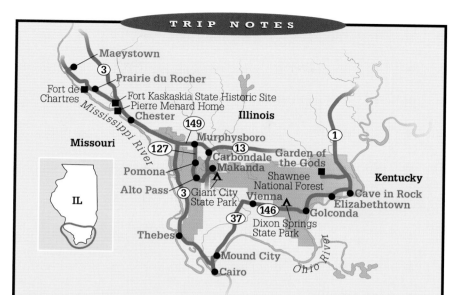

TOUR ROUTE—260 miles amid southern Illinois hill country, stopping at scenic natural areas, as well as French colonial and Civil War-era towns.

LODGINGS—Motels in Murphysboro, Carbondale and nearby Marion. Other choices: In Maeystown, the Corner George Inn, seven rooms with private baths (doubles from $69). In Prairie du Rocher, La Maison du Rocher Country Inn, two guest rooms (also hearty meals and terrific pies; doubles from $55). Near Makanda, Giant City State Park Lodge, 34 cabins and pool (doubles from $45). In Elizabethtown, the River Rose Inn Bed and Breakfast, with great views of the Ohio River (doubles from $55).

CAMPING—Lake Murphysboro State Park, west of Murphysboro. Dixon Springs State Park, Dixon Springs. Ferne Clyffe State Park,

Goreville (north of Vienna). Giant City State Park, Makanda. Horseshoe Lake Conservation Area, northwest of Cairo.

DINING—In Maeystown, Hoefft's Village Inn, country-style meals. In Elizabethtown, E'town River Restaurant, along the Ohio River.

CELEBRATIONS—At Fort Kaskaskia, a late-September music festival (618/859-3741). At Cave in Rock, Frontier Days, in June (618/289-3238). In Du Quoin (north of Carbondale), Du Quoin State Fair, late August (618/542-9373). In Murphysboro, the Apple Festival, second week in September (618/684-3200).

SIDE TRIP—The Ohio River town of Metropolis, off I-24, hosts the annual Superman Festival in June. Illinois' oldest state park, Fort Massac,

is at the east edge of town. *Contact: Metropolis Area Chamber of Commerce (800/949-5740).*

INFORMATION—*Shawnee National Forest: U.S. Forest Service, 901 S. Commercial St., Harrisburg, IL 62946 (800/699-6637). Other attractions and lodgings: Southernmost Illinois Tourism Bureau, Box 278, Ullin, IL 62992 (800/248-4373); Southwestern Illinois Tourism & Convention Bureau, 10950 Lincoln Trail, Fairview Heights, IL (800/442-1488); Carbondale Convention & Tourism Bureau, Old Passenger Depot, 111 S. Illinois Ave., Carbondale, IL 62901 (800/526-1500); Randolph County Tourism, Box 332, Chester, IL 62233 (618/826-5000, Ext. 221); Williamson County Tourism, Box 1088, Marion, IL 62959 (800/433-7399).*

north of Ellis Grove. Drive 4 miles south on State-3. A large sign points the way to your next stop.

-------- **4** --------

Fort Kaskaskia and Pierre Menard Home State Historic Sites

High above the Mississippi, Fort Kaskaskia State Historic Site once guarded Illinois' first capital city, Kaskaskia. The fort's earthen walls now protect a large park.

Pierre Menard, a wealthy businessman and Illinois' first lieutenant governor, built a French colonial mansion (open to visitors) at the foot of the bluff, just below the fort. Old Kaskaskia lies beneath the flowing river. Floodwaters destroyed the former capital in the 1880s.

Backtrack 3 miles to State-3 and continue 6 miles south on State-3, past orchards and fruit stands. Shop for fresh fruit at Colvis Orchards, off State-3.

-------- **5** --------

Chester

(Population: 8,400) Sprawling for several miles along Mississippi bluffs, this bustling county-seat town serves as the area's commercial hub. Signs direct visitors from State-3 to State Street and the modern courthouse, where you can climb a four-story staircase for a view of Missouri. Next door, the Randolph County Museum and Archives is a storehouse of French treasures from old Kaskaskia.

Drive State Street back to State-3 and drive 23 miles south to State-149. Turn east on State-149 and drive 8 miles.

-------- **6** --------

Murphysboro

(Population: 9,870) Wide, tree-lined brick streets lace many of this old town's neighborhoods, giving Murphysboro a southern flavor. Downtown thrives along State-149, and many restaurants feature barbecue as the specialty. Murphysboro is the hometown of John A. Logan, one of U.S. Grant's most trusted Civil War generals. The John A. Logan Museum tells his story.

Murphysboro and adjacent Carbondale *(see No. 10)* serve as gateways to 270,000-acre Shawnee National Forest. Get information at the U.S. Forest

Service office along State-149, as you enter Murphysboro from the west.

From State-149, drive 12 miles south on State-127.

-------- **7** --------

Pomona

(Population: 100) Stop at tiny Pomona's general store for malts and sundaes. Along Natural Bridge Road a few miles north of the store, you'll find the trailhead to Pomona Natural Bridge, an impressive stone arch, just a short walk away.

Drive 8 miles south on State 127.

-------- **8** --------

Alto Pass

(Population: 400) The giant Bald Knob Cross, a 111-foot-tall steel crucifix clad in white porcelain, stands guard over this village. Just before the turn-off that leads to the cross, visit the Alto Pass Vineyards and Winery.

Drive 2 miles southeast on County-2, then 7 miles northeast on County-1911 (Old US-51).

-------- **9** --------

Giant City State Park

Tiny Makanda *(population: 400)* in the Shawnee hills is just outside the west entrance to 3,700-acre Giant City State Park. Stop at The Makanda Boardwalk, home to crafters and artists.

The park, with a beautiful, rustic lodge, gets its name from the massive sandstone structures that nature arranged almost like a city. Rent horses here or hike the scenic trails.

Backtrack through Makanda to US-51 and drive 9 miles north.

-------- **10** --------

Carbondale

(Population: 27,000) Shops, restaurants and other businesses line Main Street (State-13) in Carbondale, a commercial hub and home of Southern Illinois University. The town's many one-way streets slice through the campus, which some consider the prettiest in Illinois.

Just east of Carbondale along State-13, pay a visit to 43,000-acre Crab Orchard Lake and National Wildlife Refuge, a favorite of anglers, campers, bird-watchers and nature lovers.

Drive 7 miles west on State-13 to State-149, backtracking through Murphysboro

Cypress trees
nearly 1,000
years old at the
Heron Pond-Little
Black Slough
Natural Area.

another 8 miles west on State-149. Drive 36 miles south on State-3, passing near Oakwood Bottoms and Pine Hills recreation areas, known for marshy terrain.

--------- **11** ---------

Thebes

(Population: 460) Once an important river town, Thebes sleeps on the banks of the Mississippi. You can visit the Thebes Courthouse, where Abraham Lincoln once practiced law and fugitive slave Dred Scott awaited the verdict that galvanized anti-slavery sentiment nationwide in the 1850s.

Drive 22 miles south through forests and marshlands on State-3. You'll pass near Horseshoe Lake, a great stop for wildlife-watching and canoeing amid cypress and tupelo swamps (150,000 Canada geese winter here).

--------- **12** ---------

Cairo

(Population: 5,930) Trapped on a spit of land at the confluence of the Mississippi and Ohio rivers, Cairo (pronounced KAY-row) became an important Union stronghold during the Civil War. Fort Defiance, now a state park, overlooks the two rivers.

Drive 4 miles north on US-51. At Mound City, drive 25 miles northeast on State-37, then 5 miles east on State-146.

--------- **13** ---------

Vienna

(Population: 1,420) This crossroads town (pronounced vie-EN-na) lies just north of the finest bayou swamp in the Midwest. The Heron Pond-Little Black Slough Natural Area brims with dense stands of swamp cypress. Hiking trails and a floating boardwalk give you a rare glimpse into the deep, dark, secret-filled swamp. Visitors can canoe at the slough and also at nearby Cache River State Natural Area, a stopover for thousands of migrating geese.

Drive 12 miles east on State-146.

--------- **14** ---------

Dixon Springs
State Park

From Vienna to the Ohio River, Shawnee National Forest dominates the landscape. Near the town of Dixon Springs, Dixon Springs State Park attracts campers, hikers and picnickers

with its moss-covered boulders, craggy outcroppings and rushing brooks.

Drive 26 miles east, then north, on State-146 through Golconda, where the downtown is a National Historic District. Just east is the Ohio River Recreational Area, with picnicking and boat rentals.

--------- **15** ---------

Elizabethtown

(Population: 500) Some of the oldest towns in Illinois, including Elizabethtown, dot the banks of the Ohio River. Bounded by Shawnee National Forest on the west and the Ohio River on the east, Elizabethtown is a postcardlike setting out of the 19th century, when the town grew to be an important iron-smelting and riverboating center. You can shop for arts and crafts at the 182-year-old Rose Hotel. Several downtown cafes put on the coffee pot before dawn and serve hearty country meals till after dark.

Drive 8 miles northeast on State-146 to State-1. Drive 2 miles south on State-1.

--------- **16** ---------

Cave in Rock

(Population: 400) This town gets its name from a massive cave hollowed into the river bluff less than a mile east. Pirates used the cave as a hideout to prey on early river travelers. The cave now is part of a state park by the same name, with hiking, caving, camping, picnicking, a lodge and restaurant. A ferry at Cave in Rock shuttles travelers across the Ohio River to Kentucky.

Drive 7 miles north on State-1 to County-1125. Drive 10 miles west to County-250E and turn north.

--------- **17** ---------

Garden of the Gods

Winding roads take you through the heart of Shawnee National Forest to reach these spectacular rock formations. After the hamlet of Karbers Ridge— actually, just a wide spot in the highway— follow the signs to Garden of the Gods.

Flagstone paths lead you through 200-million-year-old sandstone palisades, putting hikers hundreds of feet above the forest for an unmatched view, a fitting end to your Illinois hill-country weekend. ■

By Alan Guebert.

Views are grand at Garden of the Gods in Shawnee National Forest.